The Fish of Gold

And Other

Finnish Folk Tales

The Fish of Gold

And Other Finnish Folk Tales

Drawing for The Merchant's Son

Translated by Inkeri Väänänen-Jensen

Cover by Esther Feske
1906 Illustrations by Venny Soldan-Brofeldt

Dedication

I dedicate this collection of Finnish Folk tales to our four grandchildren, Tomas, Luke, Eleanor, and Hadley, to remind them that part of their heritage lies in Finland.

However, I dedicate this book not only to children, but also to people of all ages who enjoy the reading, the telling, and the reminiscing about the old folk tales from countries all over the world.

— *Inkeri Väänänen-Jensen*

ISBN 0941016-78-1
Library of Congress Number: 90-60972

Contents

A Finnish Folklore Memory

(How It May Have Been)

After the simple supper
Of rye bread and porridge,
The grandfather walked slowly to his chair
Beside the fireplace and sat down.
One by one the rest of the family,
His daughter, Aili, her husband, Aksu,
And their three children,
Ensio, Aino, and Pentti,
Sat down on the floor before him,
Eager to hear
What old Finnish folk tale
The old man might choose to tell tonight.

He can no longer read,
For his eyesight is failing,
But he remembers so well
The ancient folk tales
Told out loud around the fireplace
In the log home of his youth,
Tales of poor boys who became heroes,

Tales of beautiful princesses,
Tales of great treasures within kingdoms.
And so now,
In his strong and steady voice,
He begins,
"Once upon a time, many years ago
A poor peasant boy left his humble home
And stepped out into the world
To seek his fortune. . ."

And so *you* are invited
To turn the pages of this book
To read the tales
From those olden days,
Tales once told out loud
In many a simple farm cottage
Deep in the evergreen forests
Of Finland.
"*Olkaa hyvä*; please be seated."
For the stories are about to begin.

— *Inkeri Väänänen-Jensen*

The Fish of Gold

A poor fisherman and his wife lived in a small cottage on the shore of a lake.

Each day the old fisherman caught just enough fish in his net so the two of them barely managed to eke out a living.

One morning the fisherman went to check on his net and saw that he had caught only one fish, but it was a most peculiar one. The fisherman was puzzled, for he had never even heard tell of such a fish. It was made completely of gold; its scales were of pure gold. The fisherman was pleased and thought his wife would be sure to be delighted with such a fish.

His wife, you see, was quite ill-tempered, and very seldom did the old man do anything that pleased her, so she always scolded him and yelled at him.

The fisherman looked at the fish in his hands and was just about to drop it into his birch bark creel when the fish began to speak, "Do not take me, old Man. Please toss me back from whence I came; please toss me back into the water."

"I will not let you go!" said the old man. "For when I go home and I tell my wife about you, she will lash out at me for letting such a good catch slip out of my hands. My wife has a very bad temper."

The fish pleaded with the fisherman, "Let me go, and if you are ever in trouble, just say, 'Hip, golden Fish!' and I will come to help you, regardless of how serious your trouble is."

The old fisherman relented, and he released the fish into the water, and with an empty fishing creel he plodded toward home.

On reaching home, he told his wife about the fish he had let go. This made her so angry that she grabbed the poker and stormed in front of him, "Oh, you everlasting fool! Here you made such a good catch and yet you didn't have the sense to bring it home! You deserve a beating!"

In desperation, the old man answered, "Don't strike me, dear Wife, for the fish made me a wonderful promise."

"Well, since the fish made you such a wonderful promise, you'd better hurry back to talk with the fish again to see if he keeps his promise. Ask the fish to give us a castle, a beautiful one, which poverty will never touch."

The old man walked down to the shore, sat on the rock near the water, and called, "Hip, golden Fish!"

In a moment the fish appeared at his feet,

landing on the tips of the old man's birch bark shoes. "And what do you need, my good Man?" the fish asked.

The old man explained that his wife wanted a castle, a beautiful one, one far away from poverty.

"It is done!" said the fish, and he jumped back into the lake.

Puzzled, the old man walked toward home. But he became confused when he saw that the old cottage was nowhere to be seen, but in its stead was a beautiful, three-story castle. The old man assumed he was lost in some strange place and began to walk along the shore seeking his old cottage. But then his wife at the window of the castle saw him and sent a servant to bring the old man inside.

The castle was beautiful and for some time the old man lived there with his wife. His wife spent much of her time in bed, and had the servants wait on her, while the old man continued to keep busy working with his beloved fishing nets.

One day, when the old man was sitting alone in his room, his wife, very angry, rushed to him and shouted, "This way of life is not satisfactory; we must live better than this. Go at once to that fish of gold and tell him to give us the world's largest army and also the world's most handsome generals."

The old man began to think that perhaps all this present wealth could disappear if they greedily asked for so much more, but he did not dare to share such thoughts with his wife. So he walked obediently down to the shore. He sat on a rock and called, "Hip, golden Fish!" At once the fish appeared and flopped down on the tips of the old man's birch bark shoes.

"And what do you need, my good Man?" the fish asked, and the old man explained what his wife now wanted.

"It is done!" said the fish, and he plunged back into the lake.

The old man once again began to walk home, but then he almost fainted from shock. For there in front of the castle, a huge band was playing spirited marches, and handsomely dressed soldiers marched to the rhythm of the music. And even more handsomely attired generals directed all the soldiers.

Once again, the old man believed that by some witchery he had been carried to a strange land, and he began sadly to seek his old cottage. However, once again from the window his wife saw him and asked the soldiers to bring him inside.

The old man and his wife lived for some time in the castle with the band, the soldiers, and the generals. The old man, however, remained busy among his nets.

Once when the old man was just sitting down to eat, his wife rushed into the room, a sword in her hand, and shouted, "This will not do; this life simply will not do! I must become the mighty water spirit, who has a huge castle in the middle of the sea and who has the power to raise such a storm that everything on the surface of the earth drowns. Go at once, old Man, to that golden fish and ask for this, or I will strike you dead with this sword!"

The old man didn't dare to remain to eat his meal nor to oppose his wife. He ran as fast as he

12

could to the shore.

"Hip, golden Fish," he called, short of breath from his rush to the shore.

The fish landed again on the old man's birch bark shoes, and the old man began to explain his wife's new demands.

Angry now, and without saying a single word, the fish bounded off the old man's shoes and hit the surface of the water so hard with his tail that a six-foot high column of water shot up into the air.

"That must have been the water spirit itself," thought the old man, as discouraged, and in low spirits, he began to walk homeward. But when he reached the gate of the castle, he saw their former old cottage perched exactly where it had been before. Gone were the castle, the soldiers, and the generals.

And there on the bench sat his wife, sullen, and wearing her old patched and tattered clothes.

Hip! The golden fish did not return.

Jotaarkka

Crafty generals had maneuvered a king into a war against another king. This second king fell in battle, and his wife fled with her slain husband's white horse to a secret cottage in the wilderness. But his son was taken a prisoner by the victorious king. The son's name was Jotaarkka.

Jotaarkka sat behind bars in a prison. He sat there and wept.

The victorious king's daughter happened to walk past the barred window of the prison and she heard the prisoner crying. She felt very sorry for Jotaarkka, went to her father, and said, "Dear kind Father, I feel so bad about that boy in the prison! If you, dear Father, had died in battle I would feel bad too if I were held prisoner by my enemy. Can't Jotaarkka be set free from the prison?"

So the king freed Jotaarka from the prison, and

14

even promised him some kind of work in the castle.

The king's daughter spoke again to her father, "Since you promised him some work, give him to me as a servant. I'm sure Jotaarkka will make a good servant."

Her father answered, "You have plenty of generals as your servants. It's better that you keep them to serve you."

But his daughter declared, "I don't care for the generals; they're so cunning and sly. Please give me Jotaarkka as a servant."

So the king's daughter got Jotaarkka as her servant, and he served her for a number of years in the castle. They got along very well together.

After some years had passed, Jotaarkka said to the king's daughter, "Please give me some free time from the castle so I can go for several hours to walk around the city."

But the king's daughter replied, "Jotaarkka, I cannot permit you to go out walking alone. You might have some kind of accident. Let's go together into the city."

But Jotaarkka argued, "I, as the son of a vanquished king, cannot possibly walk with my conqueror's daughter. This is not proper, since I am the son of a defeated king. But give me a good horse, and I will ride around the city for a few hours and then return immediately."

Finally, the king's daughter agreed, and she gave Jotaarkka a good horse and off he rode to the city.

But the generals were jealous of Jotaarkka since he had become the servant of the king's daughter. When they heard that Jotaarkka had

15

ridden to the city, they rode after him. They overtook him and in a back alley they attacked him on his horse and beat Jotaarkka so badly that he fell unconscious into the alley. The generals left in a great hurry, and the horse ran back to the castle without Jotaarkka.

When the king's daughter saw Jotaarkka's horse without him, she became frightened and moaned, "What has happened to Jotaarkka? He must have been in some kind of accident."

The king's daughter jumped quickly on the horse and rode to the city, where she found Jotaarkka unconscious in the alley. She tended to him until he revived, and then they rode home together.

They continued their lives in the castle just as before, until Jotaarkka asked to be allowed to go for a walk into the forest for a little diversion.

"I do not dare to let you go walking alone," said the king's daughter. "The last time you left you had an accident. This time it could happen that you would never return. Let's go for a walk together."

"As the son of a defeated king, I cannot go for a walk with you. Just give me a good horse, and I will ride quickly into the forest and return immediately. Accidents can't happen every time."

Finally, the girl gave Jotaarkka a horse, one even finer than the one she had given him before, and Jotaarkka rode alone into the forest.

Jotaarkka reached a wide river in the forest over which a bridge had been built. Below the bridge a noisy rapids gushed downstream.

The jealous generals had again followed Jotaarkka and were now lying in ambush waiting for him. Just as Jotaarkka rode over the bridge, they rushed out of their hiding places, surrounded him and his horse and threw them both into the rapids. Then they ran away quickly.

The horse drowned in the rapids but as Jotaarkka fell, the hem of his coat caught on a pole, which was set up in the rapids as part of a trap for catching salmon. Just as Jotaarkka was dangling dangerously over the rapids, some of the king's soldiers marched over the bridge on their way to the castle. They saw a man caught on a pole, hanging over the rapids. They lifted him off the pole onto the bridge, and realized that it was none other than Jotaarkka. With great joy and with the triumphant beating of drums, they brought him to the castle. The king's daughter grasped both of Jotaarkka's hands, overwhelmed that once again he had returned from death's door. She vowed she would never again let Jotaarkka go anywhere alone.

The two were living happily within the castle when Jotaarkka once again desired to go walking somewhere.

"Let's go together since you want to go somewhere so badly. And you don't need to be ashamed to walk with your conqueror's daughter, for we will go neither to the city nor to the forest, where woodcutters and hunters move about. We can walk in our own royal park, just the two of us together."

Jotaarkka and the king's daughter walked in the royal park, where the evergreens were huge and thick, the birches tall and green. They walked for a long time; then they ran around in the park, playing like two small children. Finally, they both found they were very thirsty.

"Let's go to the spring for a drink," said the king's daughter.

But the jealous generals had secretly followed them to the park, and when they heard the two talking about going to the spring for a drink, they poured sleeping potion into the spring. In fact, they poured a very large amount of sleeping potion into the spring.

When Jotaarkka and the king's daughter drank from the spring, they immediately grew tired and felt very sleepy. All of a sudden, the king's daughter fell into a deep sleep on a small knoll on which the sun was shining. When Jotaarkka bent over to look at the king's daughter, wondering why she had so suddenly dropped off to sleep, he also fell into a deep sleep on the knoll beside her.

The generals now ran to the king and announced, "Come and see how your daughter behaves with your enemy's son, the prisoner to whom you have given freedom. Does this kind of behavior add to your dignity?"

The king hurried to the royal park, where Jotaarkka and his daughter were sleeping side by side.

The king became angry and said, "This demeans my dignity. It looks as if my enemy's son wants to become my son-in-law. That simply will not do. Both of their heads must be chopped off, since not even my daughter has considered my honor and dignity."

The generals, however, felt that death was too easy a punishment for Jotaarkka and, besides, they wanted to torment the king's daughter since she had spurned them. So, for these reasons, they told the king, "Do not chop off their heads, since they are both of royal blood. Instead, let's tie up Jotaarkka, place him in an empty boat and toss it down the rapids, and let's give the king's daughter to the dragon who lives in the high mountains."

The king agreed.

In the empty boat, Jotaarkka tumbled down the rapids, then drifted down the river. He was about to die from hunger and thirst, for he could not break out of his bonds. Finally the river current carried his boat to the shore, near a small cottage in the forest. As soon as the boat scraped against a rock on the shore, a white-haired woman came out of the cottage and looked into the boat. Lo, and behold, a young, handsome lad lay tied up in the bottom.

The white-haired woman cut Jotaarkka's bonds and asked, "Who are you? How did you get here?"

Free now, he answered, "I am Jotaarkka." And he began to tell her about himself and all that had happened to him.

The woman suddenly rushed to him, put her arms around him, and crying with joy, said, "You are my son, whom the enemy king put in prison when your father fell in battle. I escaped to this hidden cottage. You are most welcome now to your mother's house."

Jotaarkka stayed in the secret cottage with his mother, and all was well with him except that he pined for the king's daughter, who had been given to the dragon.

One evening a raven flew in, sat on the ridgepole

of the cottage, and began to talk. The old raven prattled away to himself, explaining how very sorry the king now was that he had given his daughter to the dragon. He promised to give half his castle, half of all his treasure, and half his kingdom to any general who would rescue his daughter from the dragon. But not a single general dared to attempt the task.

"Oh, how can I save the king's daughter?" cried Jotaarkka, who, with his mother, had listened to the raven's mutterings.

"Don't even consider it, my poor Boy, for you cannot save her!" his mother replied.

Jotaarkka did not respond to this, but throughout that night he lay awake in his bed, and in the morning said again, "I must rescue her!"

Jotaarkka actually became ill because he could not think of any way in which he could rescue the king's daughter from the dragon.

His mother now spoke, "Go to the king's castle wearing a disguise and watch carefully how things are going there. Find out whether the king will also promise to give you half his castle, his treasure, and kingdom. Then come back here. But do not reveal to any of the royal family who you are."

Jotaarkka, now wearing the animal-hide clothes of a poor wilderness peasant, stepped into the boat, and rowed to the king's castle. He sat, as a poor peasant, on the edge of a bench near the fireplace, warming himself and watching to see what was going on in the castle. He could see that the king was feeling very bad, and also that he was angry at the generals, since not one of them dared to go to save his daughter.

Finally, Jotaarkka said, "I am just a poor peasant, but what reward do you offer if I should rescue your daughter?"

"Half of my castle, my treasure, and my kingdom," answered the king.

Jotaarkka now spoke, "I do not want your castle, your treasure, nor your kingdom! But if you will give me your daughter, then I will rescue her!"

"So be it!" responded the king.

When Jotaarkka returned in his boat to the cottage in the wilderness, his mother asked, "How were things at the castle? Did the king promise you half his castle, his treasure, and his kingdom?"

"I did not want any of those," answered Jotaarkka. "He promised me his daughter."

His mother now said, "Go now, my Boy, toward the northwest. In the forest you will come to a huge rock, in which you will see a door. When you open this shining door, you will enter the rock's stall, where my magnificent stallion is standing on a red carpet. Approach this white horse quietly, kneel humbly before him, and say, 'Beautiful Sirkko, noble Mirkko, you served my father, you served my mother, now please serve my father's only son. Let us go together to rescue the king's daughter!'"

Jotaarkka walked from the cottage toward the northwest. In the forest he reached a huge rock with a door. He opened this shining door, entered the stall, where the stallion stood on a red carpet. He had never before seen such a beautiful horse. He was white as snow, his hair was like silk and silver, his tail and mane were as soft as new mown hay.

Very quietly, Jotaarkka knelt before the beautiful horse and said, "Beautiful Sirkko, noble Mirkko, you served my father, you served my mother, now please serve my father's only son! Let us go to rescue the king's daughter."

The horse's eyes began to sparkle and he said to Jotaarkka, "I have been well fed here, but I have been standing too long. Release me, my Boy, to try to run again."

Jotaarkka led the horse outside and as soon as the horse was in the open air, he jumped on the ground, jumped a second time, and then a third. As he jumped for the third time, huge wings opened from each of his flanks, with each wing feather like the finest silver. Like a skylark, the horse now flew into the air. For a long time he flew high above the forest, and then he returned.

"Go, my Boy, and ask your mother for food to last for three meals, ask also for the silver saddle your father used when he rode, and, finally, ask for the whip, which he also used."

Jotaarkka left and his mother gave him food for three meals, his father's silver saddle, and the whip he had used. He came back to the white horse, which said, "Place the saddle on my back, sit in it, and take the food and whip with you."

Jotaarkka placed the saddle on the horse and rose to the saddle; the lunches and whip were in the pack on his back.

Now the horse began to fly. Jotaarkka rode high through the bright air and they reached a land of radiant clouds. The clouds were fields of white and among them was a glistening well. The horse stopped at the well and said to Jotaarkka, "Dismount and give me some water to drink from the well. Eat some of your food and then drink some water from the well. I will go to eat in the green meadow on the white fields."

Jotaarkka slid off the horse onto the cloud, watered the horse, which then left to eat green grass. Jotaarkka now ate, drank water from the well, and rested on the surface of the cloud. When the horse returned from the field, Jotaarkka rose to the saddle again and they flew through the air toward their far distant goal.

They flew on and on, on silver wings; twice more they stopped to eat, to drink, and to rest among the bright fields of clouds.

Finally, they reached a high, forested mountain, and the horse said to Jotaarkka, "Dismount now, for we are at the mountain in which the king's daughter is a prisoner."

Jotaarkka slid off the horse to find the ground covered with worms, lizards, and snakes! He could not take a single step without stepping on them.

Now the horse spoke, "Jotaarkka, take out the whip from the pack on your back and strike out in all directions at the worms, lizards, and snakes. When you reach the dragon's cave, where a huge dragon is twisted three times around the cave, strike it hard on its back with your whip. When you go down into the cave, flail at each stair. The king's daughter is in that cave."

Jotaarkka walked amid all the worms, lizards, and snakes and flailed at all of them with his whip. Their eyes burned like coals, and their fiery tongues lashed out at him, but as Jotaarkka struck them, they stiffened into wooden sticks and died. In the same way, Jotaarkka also killed the huge dragon that had wrapped itself three times around the cave. As Jotaarkka walked down into the cave, he beat down on every step with his whip, and all the steps turned into dead vipers.

Jotaarkka had now reached the bottom floor of the cave, where golden lamps shone brightly from the ceiling, and where many imprisoned princesses were reclining on their couches.

As soon as Jotaarkka appeared, the king's daughter flew to him and threw her arms around his neck.

Jotaarkka said to her, "Let us leave at once."

There were, however, many others in the room, many imprisoned princesses, each of whom began to beg Jotaarkka, "Oh, dear Brother, take me away from here; take us all away from here!"

Jotaarkka answered, "Come out of the cave to the mountain. All the snakes have been killed. Go to my horse, kneel humbly before him, and ask, 'Beautiful Sirkko, noble Mirkko, take all of us away from here,' and he will, no doubt, do so."

So the young women knelt before the white horse, knelt there humbly, and politely begged, "Beautiful Sirkko, noble Mirkko, take us all to our native land."

The horse replied, "Take some food with you from the mountain. Let Jotaarkka and his friend get on my back first, then the rest of you may hang on to my mane, the saddle, the stirrups, and my legs— as many of you as can possibly find room."

So the young women gathered food into their laps and onto the horse's back, and then they hurriedly grasped whatever place they could on the horse, his mane, his locks, the knobs on the saddle, the stirrups, and his legs. As the horse spread out his wings, they shone like the sun, and they all were lifted easily into the air. The white horse flew and flew and carried Jotaarkka, the king's daughter, and the many princesses, who hung on tightly to the horse.

They flew like a swarm of bees through the air. They reached the silver fields of the clouds, where they watered the horse, and all of them ate, drank water, and rested. They repeated this two more times, and after each rest, the flying wings hastened the travelers onward.

They finally reached the king's castle, where a happy king welcomed them. There was much rejoicing, music, kissing. Jotaarkka was still wearing his peasant's disguise.

The wedding of Jotaarkka and the king's daughter was now to take place. All the released princesses were to serve as bridesmaids, wearing white dresses adorned with flowers.

Jotaarkka spoke to the king, "Your Majesty, please allow me to go into the forest to bring my mother to the wedding."

The king gave him permission and even provided a golden boat in which Jotaarkka's mother could ride along the river from her forest cottage.

When Jotaarkka's mother stood before the king, he was startled and asked, "Who are you?"

The white-haired woman replied, "I am the widow of your enemy, whom you killed in battle."

"And who are you?" the king then asked Jotaarkka.

"Jotaarkka!" he answered and took off his peasant's clothes. And there he stood, dressed in garments of silver, a handsome, royal prince.

"Take everything, Jotaarkka. Take everything, Jotaarkka's mother. Take my treasure, my castle, my kingdom. Then we can live in peace," said the king.

Jotaarkka and his mother accepted, and now the wedding flutes and drums began to play. The white horse led the bridal party. The cover on his back was a crimson cloth, trimmed in silver.

The Old Woman and Her Lucky Rabbit's Foot

A poor old woman made twig brooms in the forest. One rainy day she spent the whole day making the brooms. When night began to fall, she was very tired and drenched to the skin.

"Oh my, oh my," she sighed to herself. "If, for just once in my life, I could get what I wished for, I know exactly what that would be. I would wish for a brand new cottage, and also that I would always have bread and coffee on the table of that cottage for as long as I live. Then I would not have to slave at making these twig brooms, which bring in so little money."

The old woman sighed again, and suddenly a handsome woodsman appeared before her. From his pouch of badger skin, the woodsman drew out a rabbit's foot, gave it to the old woman and said, "Here, old Woman, take this rabbit's foot and when you get home, just brush the table with it and make a wish. Your wish will come true. But remember this, you have only two wishes."

The woodsman whistled for his dogs and disappeared into a grove of birches.

The poor old woman walked home with her load of twig brooms over her shoulder and the rabbit's foot in her pocket. She dropped her load of brooms beside the door, went to sit at the head of her table, and said, "Now my days of worry are over since I have this rabbit's foot."

27

But then she began to have some doubts. "Could it be that the handsome woodsman was just deceiving me, a poor old woman? How is it possible that with this rabbit's foot I can get whatever I wish for? I must test it out."

So the old woman decided to wish for something foolish and impossible to test whether the wish would be fulfilled. She didn't believe it would. She sat at the head of the table, took the rabbit's foot from her pocket, brushed it over the table and laughing to herself, said, "Let something utterly foolish happen. Let this cottage turn upside down!"

Presto! The old woman felt herself tossed into the air. She was turned topsy-turvy. At the same time she saw that her cottage was upside down, the floor was the ceiling and the ceiling was the floor. Her stove pipe was touching the ground, and the trap door on the floor was now a chimney.

The woman shook with fright. "Oh dear, oh dear, that I should make such a foolish wish! Now I have only one wish left, since the woodsman said that I have only two wishes. What is the best thing for me to wish? What else but that this wretched, yet dear, cottage be turned right side up again."

She crawled to her table, brushed the top with her rabbit's foot and said, "Let this cottage return to its former condition and right side up."

Presto! The cottage was exactly as it had been before and the woman was again sitting at the head of the table.

"What have I, poor Woman, done?"

She was thoroughly frightened by now and remarked, "I should have wished for a new cottage for myself, with food and coffee on the table for as long as I live. But now I can wish for nothing more, since my two wishes have come true."

And that poor old woman remained poor. She did not get her new cottage nor food and coffee on the table for as long as she would live. She remained a maker and seller of twig brooms for the rest of her life.

The Emperor's Debt

A good-natured widower had a son whom he had raised and supported for 15 years with much work and worry.

One day the boy called down to his father from the warm shelf above the fireplace where he had been loafing, "You know, both of us ought to get married. It is no longer right that we live without wives."

To this the father answered, "We can't afford to get married. We have no money."

But the boy said, "Go to the emperor and ask him for money so we both can get married."

The father went in a humble mood to the emperor and said, "Good, kind Emperor, give me money so my son and I can both get married."

This angered the emperor and he snapped, "Shame on you, you Blockhead! You come to ask for money from the emperor? Don't you know that the emperor *never* gives money to a peasant? It's the other way around. The peasant must pay heavy taxes to the emperor.

"As punishment, tomorrow you must give the correct answers to two riddles I am going to ask you. And also tomorrow you are to make up a riddle which none of the royal family has ever heard. If you cannot do both of these, I will have your head chopped off! To think that you came to ask the emperor for money!"

Regretting that he had even gone to the emperor, the man walked home. From the top of the hearth, his son called out, "How much money did the emperor give you?"

His father answered, "Not a penny! And he commanded me to come back to him tomorrow to answer some riddles. If I cannot give the right answers to two riddles and also make up one riddle that the royal family has never heard, he will have my head chopped off."

"That's one head that's in debt to death," mused the boy, who then turned over on his side and fell asleep again.

The next morning as the father was setting out to go to the emperor, the boy said, "I think I'll come with you."

The boy clambered down from the shelf above the hearth, washed his face, and went with his father to see the emperor.

When they had arrived at the emperor's palace and stood before him, the emperor asked the first riddle of the boy's father. It was, "What is the most precious thing on earth?"

Then the boy asked, "May not the son answer for his father since the father has raised him for 15 years with much work and worry?"

The emperor answered, "Yes, he may."

And the boy answered the emperor's first riddle for his father, "For the starving, bread; for the weary, sleep. These are the most precious things on earth."

"Well answered!" said the emperor. "I thought you would say money for the poor and a wife for one who has no wife are the most precious things on

31

earth. For I know that you and your father are eager to get married. And now here is the second riddle. It is, 'What do you, my boy, and I, the Emperor, do at the same time?'"

The boy asked again, "May the son answer for his father since the father has raised him for 15 years with great work and worry?"

The emperor answered again, "You may."

And the boy answered the second riddle, "You, the Emperor, and I, the boy, grow older at the same time."

"Well done!" said the emperor. "I thought you would answer, 'I, the boy, and you, the Emperor, both just loaf about at the same time. I can see, my Boy, that you are very lazy since you have permitted your father to support you for 15 years with much work and worry."

To the father the emperor now said, "Up to this point, your son has rescued you. But now, in your turn, you tell us a riddle which our royal family has never heard. After that we will see what happens."

Beforehand, the emperor had advised his family thus: "Regardless of what the old man tells you, you are to answer, 'Yes, we have certainly heard that.'"

Now the boy again asked the emperor, "May the son present the riddle instead of the father since the father has supported the boy for 15 years with much work and worry?"

And the emperor answered, "Well, ask your riddle then."

So the boy told this riddle to the royal family. "For 15 years my father, with much work and worry, saved his money and finally he had fifty-thousand gold pieces. Then my father loaned these fifty-thousand gold pieces to the emperor. The emperor promised that today he would pay off the loan to my father. You have all heard this?

"Yes, we have certainly heard that," responded the family with one voice.

"Ahaa!" said the boy, turning toward the emperor. "Please pay off your debt of fifty-thousand gold pieces to my father just as you had promised. The members of your own family stand as witnesses."

At first the emperor was very angry, but then he began to laugh and requested that the boy's father be given a large sack full of money. He said, "Take these fifty-thousand gold pieces since you have saved them for 15 years with such great work and worry. And now you'd better hurry home and get married!"

The father and his son hurried home and both of them did get married.

The Wise Wife

Once upon a time there was a rich man who had such a beautiful wife that one more beautiful could not be found on either land or sea. She was so unusually lovely that stars twinkled on her shoulders and the moonlight shone on her brow. The rich man was very happy.

This woman said to her husband, "Keep it a secret that you have such a beautiful wife. Do not talk or boast about me to anyone."

To this the man agreed.

As it happened, the rich man went into the city where the king lived, and he was invited to a banquet at the castle. Everything there was so magnificent and glittering; the floors were of silver, the columns of gold, and the ceilings of precious gems. The man sat with the royal family at a silver table. They all ate and drank; the rich man drank perhaps a little too much. The king's daughter sat at the head of the table, and she was certainly beautiful with a gold crown on her head. Her hair was of the purest gold.

The king began to praise his daughter, "My daughter is the most beautiful person on earth. There is not a more lovely woman under God's blue heaven than my daughter. Let us drink a toast to her!"

The king's guest, the rich man, was annoyed when the king called his daughter the world's most beautiful woman. He began to think that he really ought to praise his wife at least a little, for she certainly was a hundred times more beautiful than the king's daughter.

The rich man now responded to the king's request, "I can certainly drink a toast to the daughter of our most gracious king, but I question whether she is the world's most beautiful woman."

This alarmed everyone at the table and angered the king, "I demand an explanation. Is not my daughter the most beautiful woman under God's heaven?"

It was now necessary for the rich man to respond immediately and he said, "My gracious king's daughter is beautiful, but my wife is twice as beautiful. She's so lovely that stars twinkle on her shoulders, and the moonlight shines on her brow. And she is waiting for me at home."

The king turned angrier, threw his rich guest into prison and said, "She can wait for you a long time. Why did you come here to insult my daughter?"

The man sat in the dark prison at the base of the tower, where only at twilight did a few rays of light manage to penetrate the darkness, and where hungry rats scurried about.

When the rich man's wife heard about the quarrel between the king and her husband and that her husband had been thrown into prison, she began to wail and cry. When she had cried long enough, she began to think about ways in which she could rescue her husband from the prison.

She now devised a plan. She spent a great deal of money: She ordered the tailoring of a man's handsome clothes, clothes fit for a prince. She cut her hair short and then dressed in the new clothes. Behold, there he stood, a handsome, royal prince, a hat of plumed feathers on his head, a sword at his side, and shining spurs on his boots. "He" was the rich man's wife.

She bought a carriage of glass and four splendid horses, hired a coachman, stepped into the carriage, and asked to be driven to the king's castle.

When she arrived at the castle, she explained that she was the prince from a neighboring kingdom, who had come to woo the king's daughter.

The king was pleased, for the suitor had arrived in such a grand style. His daughter was even more pleased, since her suitor was so handsome that there was no one like him under heaven. The sun shone on his brow and stars sparkled on his shoulders.

The king entered the courtyard, bowing to this false prince. He led him into the castle, gave him food and drink, and treated him most royally and promised his daughter to him as his wife immediately.

His daughter was overjoyed to get such an attractive husband, for they would then be the world's most beautiful couple.

But the king's mother began to have some doubts, and she whispered to the king, "Do not give your daughter to that stranger, for he is not a man; he is a woman."

"Don't be ridiculous," said the king. "He is most certainly a man and, besides that, he is also the world's best man."

However, the old queen would not yield, but said, "Invite the stranger for a bath in the sauna and station guards to watch. Then you will find out that she *is* a woman."

Finally, the king consented and said to the visiting prince, "Before we begin the wedding celebration I will have the sauna heated so, my young Hero, you will be cleansed."

The rich man's wife immediately understood that she would be spied upon, and pondered on how to escape from her awkward predicament. She went for a walk in the royal park, which was alive with all kinds of small forest animals, weasels, rabbits, martens, squirrels. She slipped a weasel into one of her pockets and a squirrel into another.

She returned to the king's courtyard and went to the sauna. A wide, red cloth had been hung all the way from the castle to the door of the sauna. She walked along this cloth to the sauna. The sauna itself was made of gold, and the top of the firebox was filled with precious stones. Sweet mead was thrown on the stones to create the steam.

As the false prince began to undress, from her pocket she released the squirrel, which began to run about the sauna wall. The guards watched the antics of the squirrel while she completed her bath.

The king questioned the guards who had been on duty, "Was our guest a man or a woman?"

"It was a man," they answered, they who had watched only the squirrel during the duration of the bath.

The king went to his mother and said, "Mama dear, see what nonsense you have been guilty of; our guest is a man."

37

But his mother still insisted that their guest was a woman and requested that new watchmen be stationed in the sauna.

The king now sent his guest once again to the sauna and also sent better watchmen with her. But as the guest undressed, she released the weasel to run along the sauna wall. The weasel darted so quickly about the wall that the watchmen were kept so busy watching the weasel that they forgot to notice whether the bather was a man or a woman.

Again the king asked the watchmen, "The prince certainly is not a woman?"

The watchmen answered, "The prince is a man."

But the king's mother insisted even more strongly that she was right.

"Let me serve as the watchman," she requested.

"What next!" the king replied. "I wouldn't believe you even if I made you the watchman. You are getting old, and your eyesight is not the best. I will now hold a grand celebration for my daughter and the prince from our neighboring kingdom."

There was nothing more his mother could do, and so the celebration began.

It was a great event. For five weeks the peasants in the kingdom were guests in the royal park, where the birch trees grew apples, the evergreens provided raisins, and the junipers produced coffee beans. For five weeks they celebrated in the large hall, and of all those in attendance, the bridegroom was the most dazzling.

On the last day of the celebration, the bridegroom said to the king, "Only once in his lifetime does a proper fellow have a wedding. At that time, he wishes to share his joy with even those who are the least desirable. Please release all the prisoners from the jail so they can at least see this celebration."

The king agreed with this suggestion and freed all the prisoners from the jail. Among them, of course, was the rich man.

The wedding march now began and as it moved from the castle through the country villages, 100 musicians walked in front of the procession and 100 more walked behind. The bride rode in a carriage made of glass and the bridegroom rode on a prancing, red horse. The peasants on both sides of the road bowed deeply as the two passed by. The young bridegroom scanned the kneeling onlookers, seeking her husband. And suddenly there he stood, his hat in his hand, in prisoner's garb, the rich man between two thieves.

"That bridegroom certainly looks like my wife!" the rich man thought to himself. "But I know I will never see my wife again!" He sighed, and wept.

Just then the bridegroom rode near the rich man, rode up close to him, and said, "I am your wife and I have come to rescue you. Jump quickly on the horse and let us escape. This is the king's best horse; I selected him from the stall myself."

Frightened at first, the man was overcome with joy, jumped at once on the horse's back behind his wife, and they spurred the horse onward. They continued to spur on the horse while arrows flew all around them. The people scattered before them as they rode, and they managed to escape. As they rode along, however, they were pursued with much shouting and yelling. A thousand soldiers chased them, but suddenly the horse and its two riders disappeared into the forest.

In tears, the king's daughter went to her father, "Why, Father, did you promise me to a man who ran away and took a prisoner with him?"

The king's mother replied, "He was not a man. I knew all the time that he was a woman."

One of the peasants said, "It was a woman, but she was the most beautiful woman under heaven. The sun shone on her brow, and heaven's stars twinkled on her shoulders."

"She was the rich man's wife," remarked the king.

"Yes, yes," said the old queen. "There is a saying, 'Long hair, a weak mind'. Isn't that the truth?"

"But her hair was cut short," answered the king.

The rich man henceforth lived with his wife in a cottage in the middle of the forest, and never again did he venture into the courtyard of the king.

The Namesake Trees, or The Mouse Bride

Once upon a time a farmer had three sons, each of whom had a tree planted and named after him. When the sons had grown to manhood, all three wished to get married. Their father now asked each son to chop down his namesake tree. In whichever direction each tree fell, then the son was to go in that direction to seek his bride.

One fine day, all three sons chopped down their namesake trees. The oldest son's tree fell toward a wealthy farmhouse. The second son's tree also fell toward a large house. But the youngest son's tree fell toward the thick, dark forest.

Without hesitating, each boy started walking in the direction in which his tree had fallen. The two older boys walked toward houses familiar to the family. But the youngest walked into the forest, not knowing what he would find.

After he had walked for many hours, he spied a small cottage in the wilderness. He walked toward it and knocked on the door. When no one answered his knock, he opened the door and stepped inside. The house was empty. All who had once lived there had evidently left. Only a small mouse was sitting on the table. When the boy saw no one in the house, he was filled with sadness, and turned to leave. But the mouse on the table called to him, "Why are you so sad, my fair young Stranger?"

41

"Because," the boy answered, "I came here looking for a bride, whom my father sent me to seek, but I did not find her."

"Marry me!" the mouse cried.

"Why, you're not even a human! How can I possibly marry you?" asked the boy.

"Marry me anyhow," urged the mouse. "You won't regret it!"

"Well, I suppose I might as well," answered the boy. He did not say any more, but in great sadness he left the mouse's cottage and walked back home.

His brothers had already reached home, and they immediately asked this late-arriving brother, "And what did you find in the forest?"

"I found a good one," he answered and with that, he went unhappily to bed.

The next morning the father called all his sons together and asked each one if he had found a bride. The two older brothers each said, "Yes, I have found a good bride," but the youngest brother, who had become engaged to a mouse, did not boast about his success, but said only, "I have also found a bride."

"Now you must all go to get gifts from your future brides," said the father, adding, "You must each get a loaf of bread from your bride so we can see which one bakes the best bread."

The boys left immediately on their errands. The two older ones walked to the houses where their brides lived. But the youngest left to get his loaf of bread from a mouse.

He had barely stepped into the cottage, when the mouse asked, "What are you looking for now, my Dear? Have you come to marry me?"

"I came to get something from you," the boy answered with a short laugh. "My father has requested each son to bring a loaf of bread from his bride, to discover which one bakes the best bread."

As soon as she heard this, the mouse took a tiny reindeer bell and ringing it, gathered all her mice together. She asked them to bring the very best of their wheat grains to her. In no time at all, they were all back, each bringing grains of wheat. Out of them the mouse made a loaf of bread for her suitor. The boy, although he was puzzled as to just how the mouse could make such a loaf, thanked her, and left for home with the loaf under his arm.

The next morning, the father asked his sons to show their gifts, and each brought his bread to be examined. Neither of the older brothers had bread made out of such good flour as the youngest one's. The oldest son's bread was made of heavy rye, the middle son's loaf was of barley, but the youngest son's bread was of the purest wheat.

The father, of course, saw the differences in the breads, but did not say anything. He now gave his sons another task, saying "Go now, my Sons, and bring me a piece of cloth your bride has woven, so I can judge which bride is the most skillful weaver."

So the boys went once again to their brides as their father had requested. The youngest son walked to the mouse's house in the forest.

As she had asked before, the mouse asked again, "What, my Dear, are you looking for now?"

"My father has requested that I bring him a piece of cloth which you have woven. That is what I am seeking now," answered the boy.

"Is that so?" said the mouse, and she reached for the reindeer bell, rang it, and all the other mice

43

rushed to her just as they had before. As they gathered before her, she asked each mouse to bring her as quickly as possible the very best piece of linen thread each one had. With such a request, the mice left running, and it was not long before they all returned, bringing their mistress as many pieces of linen thread as she could possibly need.

And now the work began: some mice spun, others reeled, some wove, until in one night they had the whole piece of cloth completed.

The mouse bride took the cloth and put it into a nutshell— whatever she could fit into the shell— and placed the nutshell into her suitor's hand. He thanked the mouse for the gift and went on his way.

All three brothers reached home at the same time, and their father asked if all had received some cloth. The two older brothers showed their father the cloth they had brought. One's was cotton twill, and the other's was coarse linen. But the youngest son did not wish to even show his cloth since there was so little of it.

But his father insisted, "So, where is your cloth? You must also show your bride's handiwork!"

"I believe I do have a small piece of cloth," this last son finally answered, as he took the nutshell out of his pocket and handed it to his father.

The other two boys burst out laughing when they saw the container in which their youngest brother was carrying his cloth. But when their father opened the nutshell, pulled out the cloth, and spread it out, it turned out to be fifty yards of the finest and most delicate linen of a kind that had never been seen before.

Well, the two older brothers were jealous when they saw how fine and exquisite their youngest brother's cloth was compared to theirs. But what could they do? They were, of course, also very angry, but they dared not show their anger, for they feared their father.

The next morning the father called the boys to him and said, "Go now, my Sons, and fetch your brides here so we can see who has chosen the best one."

All three left immediately to fulfill their father's request. The two older ones walked to the homes of their brides just as they had done before. The youngest son went to the mouse in the cottage and said, "My father wishes to see you."

"Well, since he wants to see me, let's go!" answered the mouse, and she harnessed five black mice to a carriage made of nutshells and climbed up and seated herself in the carriage. The bride was now ready to go.

But the boy, when he saw this peculiar arrangement, said to the mouse, "How can I possibly bring you like this to my home— my brothers will laugh at us, and my father will be very angry."

"Don't let all this disturb you! Let's get started on our journey."

And so they departed. The mouse drove the carriage in great style, and the boy walked beside it.

On the way to the boy's home, they had to cross a bridge spanning a river. Just as they reached the bridge, they met a man, who stopped to stare at this odd mouse caravan and said, "What kind of peculiar traveling band is this?" After saying this, he kicked the carriage and all the mice into the river. The boy remained on the bridge, grief-stricken.

As he stood there, out of the river rose five pitch-black horses drawing a golden carriage in which sat a lovely girl.

Driving on the bridge, the girl halted the horses and invited the boy into the carriage. The boy, amazed, stepped up into the carriage and sat beside the girl.

She started the carriage rolling again and spoke to her companion, "Don't you know me anymore? You became engaged to me while I lived as a mouse. I am by birth the daughter of a king, but an evil witch laid a spell on me, forcing me to live as a mouse until some boy would come to offer me marriage, and another boy would toss me into the water to die. Well, since you became engaged to me, and I was also thrown into the river, the spell has been broken and I am saved. I sit beside you now as a young girl."

"Let us go at once and celebrate our wedding!" shouted the boy and in the handsome carriage he rode home with his bride.

His two brothers, who with their brides had just arrived, could not believe their eyes when they saw their youngest brother drive in proudly with handsome, black horses and a magnificent carriage. They were even more astonished when they saw his beautiful bride, whose equal in beauty they had never seen before.

When the wedding celebrations had ended, the young boy left his father's house and drove with his bride to her own house, which was now changed into a magnificent castle.

All those left behind had stared with open mouths as the two of them drove away.

The Golden Spinning Wheel

A king once had a beautiful daughter, but she was so arrogant that a more arrogant girl had never before been seen or even heard of. Many suitors came to ask for her hand, but not one of them was good enough for her, regardless of how good they might have been. The king's daughter ridiculed all her suitors.

However, not far away, a rich emperor ruled over his empire, and his son, who was unusually handsome and considered by everyone as a most desirable young man, decided to try to win the king's daughter.

The emperor's son drove to the king's court in a carriage of glass drawn by three white horses. He was welcomed warmly at the castle. The young daughter of the king also pretended to be friendly to the emperor's son, but every now and then she made fun of him and did not respond in any way to his offer of marriage.

This kind of behavior began to irritate the emperor's son, but something even worse was about to happen to him. When he went to the stable to check on his horses, he did not even recognize them until they began to whinny at him. For, you see, the white horses had been smeared with dark color; the king's daughter had permitted them to be daubed with tar.

"I'll teach her a lesson!" stormed the emperor's son.

He remained at the castle for a few more days and courted the king's daughter. However, she continued to ridicule him. When the emperor's son went again to the stable to look at his tarred horses, he discovered that the face hair, the forelock, and the mane of his very best horse had been shaved off. Written with chalk on its forehead was, "Did the prince bring his horse to us for barbering?"

The king's daughter herself had shaved the horse and written the message on its forehead.

This really angered the emperor's son. He harnessed his horses to his carriage, waved good-bye as he passed the castle, and drove home. But he decided then and there that he would make the king's daughter his wife, regardless of what it might cost.

After some time had passed, one evening a beggar appeared at the door of the men servants' cottage of the castle. He carried a large box on his back and told the men that he had a spinning wheel, which, whenever he turned it, made 10 cuckoos jump on the wheel and sing all kinds of marches and songs for dancing.

It so happened that the princess's maids heard the man's story, and they ran right away to tell her, "Some kind of beggar has come into the hired men's cottage, and he has a spinning wheel in a box, so that when he turns it, 10 cuckoos jump on the wheel and sing all kinds of marches and songs for dancing."

"Bring that spinning wheel here!" commanded the king's daughter.

The maids ran to take the spinning wheel away from the man, but he retorted, "If you as much as touch this spinning wheel, the 10 cuckoos will turn into hawks, which will then pluck out your eyes! Nor will the spinning wheel sing if I myself do not turn it. But if the king's daughter wishes to hear the music, let her come to the men servants' cottage. Then I will spin it for her."

The maids ran to their mistress and told her what the man had said.

"He wants me to come to the men servants' cottage? I should say not!" shouted the king's daughter, and she struck out at her maids. "Furthermore, I don't care one bit about that old spinning wheel."

But the next morning, her maids came and told their mistress, "The wheel is spinning now and 10 cuckoos are jumping on the wheel and singing all kinds of marches and dancing songs, and everyone is dancing."

"Won't that man promise to come here to play?" asked the king's daughter.

"No, he won't," answered her maids. "He won't come here. You will have to come to the men servants' cottage to listen."

The king's daughter wanted very much to see and hear the spinning wheel, so she said to her maids, "If I do what that beggar says, you must be sure not to tell anyone; otherwise I will get into trouble. The men servants will have to be asked to leave their cottage so they will not be able to see me."

The men servants were driven from the cottage, and the king's daughter ran very swiftly to the musician.

The musician began to spin the wheel; the cuckoos jumped; the music poured forth as the cuckoos sang all kinds of marches and dancing songs. At first the princess listened with her nose in the air, but the longer she listened, the happier she became, and finally she even wanted to dance. But the man suddenly stopped all the music.

"Turn the wheel some more," she asked.

"Enough is enough," the man answered and would not play any more.

The next morning the king's daughter said to her maids, "Run and ask the man to come here to spin the wheel so we can dance!"

The maids ran to him and asked him to come to the castle, but he refused. He sent word with them that if the king's daughter would come and dance with the men servants, then he would be happy to provide the music.

"How awful! To even think of my dancing with the men servants! I really don't care at all about dancing, anyhow," said the king's daughter.

But the next morning she said to her maids, "I really feel sorry for that poor beggar. What if, just for fun, I should take a few turns with the men servants?"

The king's daughter went to the cottage, and danced there with the men servants for half the day.

When news of this reached the king, he grew angry, and said, "This is the most astonishing behavior. My daughter hops around dancing with the men servants and yet she rejects suitors of royal blood."

The king scolded his daughter, "So you hop around with my men servants and yet you turn away royal suitors. I will teach you a lesson! What brought you to the men's cottage in the first place?"

"The spinning wheel," his daughter answered. "A man came here with a golden spinning wheel and when he spins it, 10 cuckoos jump and sing all kinds of marches and dancing tunes. All this makes a person want to dance. However, the wheel will not provide music unless the man himself spins it. The man refuses to come into the castle to spin the wheel; nor will he even spin it in the servant's cottage unless I dance with the men servants."

"I don't care about his spinning! He can just march out of here tomorrow morning!" said the king.

All night long the king's daughter worried because the man and his spinning wheel had to leave the next day.

In the morning, she went to her father and pleaded, "Please don't drive that man away! I would like to hear the spinning wheel and dance. But I promise not to go again to the men servants' cottage to dance. When the man begins to play, I will open the window in my room, listen to the music, and dance in my room with my maids. I will die of grief, if I do not hear the spinning wheel!"

The king replied, "All right then. Let the man remain here, but he'd better play his music only during mealtime, so the servants can put in full working days. But remember, you are not to go to dance with the men servants."

That very day, the king's daughter opened the window in her room and when the man played in the cottage, she began to dance in her room with her maids. However, when the man noticed that the king's daughter had begun to dance, he stopped playing, put his spinning wheel in its box, and did not take it out all day.

This not only angered the king's daughter, but she also became depressed.

The next morning her maids ran to her and said, "The man has now gone behind the stable and plays his music there. He says he will never again come to the cottage to play."

"Oh, how cruel of him!" moaned the king's daughter.

She heard no music that day and did not dare to go to listen to him.

At the end of the day, the maids ran to the king's daughter and reported, "Will wonders never cease! That man has a large doll behind the stable, a doll that blows into a horn. It also sings and tells all kinds of fairy tales and fables."

"What's the doll like?" the king's daughter asked.

"Well, what it does is this: It blows on its horn

and then sings songs and tells all kinds of tales and fables."

This kind of explanation did not satisfy the king's daughter.

"I don't suppose he would bring the doll here," the king's daughter said. "Let him keep it then. I don't really care about it anyhow."

But the more her maids talked about the doll, the sadder she became.

"Go and ask the man nicely if he will sell his doll. And be sure to ask him how many sacks of gold he wants for it."

That man would not sell the doll.

"Don't talk to me any more about that doll. I'm tired of listening to your talk about it!" shouted the king's daughter to her maids as they kept on talking about the doll.

But three days later, the king's daughter said, "I just cannot forget that doll. How could I get to see it?"

"Just go to see it," the maids joyfully replied.

"But my father will not permit it."

"What of it? Let's go at night. You won't be any the worse for such a visit."

The king's daughter was delighted. "I won't be any the worse for going. A person doesn't get any worse if she looks at a doll behind the stable. But don't tell anyone about my visit there."

When darkness fell, the princess and her maids slipped furtively behind the stable. The man was there and the doll was blowing into a large horn, and then it sang romantic love songs and told remarkable folk and fairy tales.

The king's daughter waited through the whole

53

of the next day and when it was dark, she went behind the stable to listen again to the love songs and the wonderful stories.

But just as her enjoyment was at its height, the king burst out of a corner of the stable shouting, "So here you are again, Daughter. Didn't I warn you about coming to the men servants' cottage, and now you come to the stable every evening! I do not care to have you come home, for you will never develop into a dependable person. You can just march with this doll's dancing master to all the world's fairs and make music for dancing!"

The king would not relent, even though his daughter and her maids all pleaded on bended knees. He would not even permit his daughter to return home for the night.

"Oh dear, oh dear, what will happen to me now that my father is sending me away from home?" she cried. "You will have to support me since you are the one who enticed me!" she snapped to the man.

But the man answered, "Don't you snap at me, or I will leave you here all alone, and what will you, Mademoiselle, do then? You will have to behave yourself if you want a place to sleep and food to eat. I'm leaving and you can follow right behind me."

The king's young daughter was now very angry, bitter, and also sad, to be ordered about in such a way, but she had no choice but to follow behind the man.

They walked for a long time through the darkness along muddy roads. The king's daughter's white, thin leather shoes became soiled and ripped; broken branches and twigs tore at her feet. She grew tired, but the man just shouted back to her,

"Can't you walk a little faster? You certainly are a lazy one!"

The king's daughter's heart was bitter and she snapped back at him, "I am not your slave! I'm not going to come with you! I'll just stay right here!"

But the man just laughed and said, "Stay here then, if that's what you want!"

And he continued on his way without stopping.

The king's daughter planned to stay, but then she began to fear being left alone and thought to herself, "Oh, I have no home, or anything! I'll have to obey him until I learn how to get along by myself. When that time comes, I'll quit obeying him!"

And she began to follow him.

They walked for a long time until they reached a large swamp.

The man said, "This is a large swamp, full of water, with a narrow footbridge over it. I will now have to let my treasures sink into the swamp in order to carry you across. You can't possibly manage to stay on that narrow footbridge."

The girl responded, "I can so manage!" And she began to walk across, but slipped immediately into the swamp.

The man called, "I told you you wouldn't be able to stay on the footbridge. You evidently only know how to dance, and that only on a smooth floor. Goodness, what trouble you are causing me! Now I have to leave my expensive spinning wheel and my doll to sink into the swamp just to save you!"

The man threw his box into the swamp and lifted the girl into his arms. He carried her across the footbridge and said, "You got your lovely dress wet and dirty in the swamp. Even your shoes are

55

ruined. How will we now pay for our nights' lodgings and our food? I cannot pay since I left my expensive spinning wheel and doll behind. Goodness, what trouble you are causing me!"

"Leave me. Perhaps you can still rescue your valuables," cried the princess.

The man answered, "Is that right? However, a person's life is more valuable to me than all that equipment, a little more valuable, I must say."

"Thank you," said the king's daughter.

At midnight they reached a small village and stopped at an inn. The man left the girl in the entry and said he himself would go inside to ask for food and lodging.

Inside, the man poured many gold coins on the table before the innkeeper, and said, "When my friend comes in to ask for food, please give her only two dried herrings and moldy bread. If she begins to get angry, you must accuse her of being a thief. Then in the morning, you must demand payment from us for staying here. If you do not do as I say, know that I am the son of the emperor, and I will send a hundred soldiers to attack you!"

Taken aback, the innkeeper promised to do as he was told, and the man returned to the entry and said to the king's daughter, "We were not promised any food and lodging. You take your turn now and go inside to ask, for you at least have better clothes than I. Perhaps they will give you something since you look better than I do."

The king's daughter went to the innkeeper and asked, "Do you have an evening meal and a night's lodging for us?"

"Of course, if you can pay for it," answered the

innkeeper, and he brought her a crust of moldy bread and two dried herrings.

"For shame! I am a king's daughter and do not eat herring!" she shouted.

"What? A king's daughter?" ridiculed the innkeeper. "So you are a king's daughter! You are also probably a thief, for how else would you have such fine clothing? Wait a while, I'll get the constable, and we'll find out whether you're a princess!"

In tears, the king's daughter returned to the man waiting in the entry and in anger told him that she would not eat that awful food even if not eating it meant dying.

The man answered, "I will certainly eat it. One simply has to. This sort of thing often happens to the poor."

He went into the inn, leaving the king's daughter in the entry— very hungry.

In the dining room, the man ordered the table filled with the finest food. He ate and drank with great enjoyment. He then returned to the princess and said, "I am now satisfied, and, thank God, we even got a place to sleep for the night. Let us go to the hay barn to sleep."

There was nothing for the exhausted princess to do but to go to the hay barn. She wept a long time and, still weeping, and also very hungry, she finally fell asleep. But she had barely fallen asleep when it was morning, and someone was pounding and banging on the door. The innkeeper was there, pounding and shouting, "I don't know whether those vagabonds are still here. Just so they haven't run off without paying their bill. Hey, wake up and pay your bill, you beggars and princesses!"

"Now we must run. They demand payment and we don't have anything to pay with!" said the man, and he began to draw the girl outside.

"I haven't the strength to run!" cried the princess.

"Then I'll have to carry you; otherwise they will steal your shoes and your dress, the only things we still have that are of any value."

The man hoisted her on his back and they fled, with the innkeeper, shouting and screaming, hot on their heels. They ran for a long time, and the innkeeper finally stopped chasing them.

The man slid the princess off his back and she said, "Thank you! I would have been very cold without my shoes and my dress."

"Well, you may still get very cold. I cannot keep you with me much longer, for you are too arrogant. Beggars have to be humble and not behave as you did at the inn."

And what do you know? When they reached the next inn, she ate the hard bread and two dried herrings, and was satisfied.

They walked again for a long time, and the princess did all the begging for them. They finally reached the emperor's kingdom. The man now said, "You have probably by now managed to learn how to get along by yourself. I am going into the emperor's city to look for work. You and I will now have to go our separate ways."

This frightened the king's daughter and she pleaded, "Do not, good Man, leave me alone. What will happen to me, for I have not yet learned how to get along by myself."

The man answered, "Well, if you will marry me,

then you can remain with me, and together we will try to get along somehow."

The princess agreed, and the man left for the city to look for work and told her he would soon return.

The man went directly to the emperor's castle and, as the emperor's son, he was welcomed with great rejoicing. While at the castle, he ate and drank, and rested for a long time. At last he returned to the king's daughter and said, "The times are hard! I begged and pleaded for a long time before I finally got work. I got a job in the emperor's clay pottery. I have to work long days in order to earn our daily food. Only at night will I be able to return to you. But we have been given a fine house; come and look at your new home."

The emperor's son led the king's daughter to the outskirts of the city to a wretched hut not much larger than a doghouse, and he said, "Here, then, is our home. In the evening I will bring you food, but during the day you will have to do without."

"Thank you!" replied the king's daughter.

The emperor's son stayed in the city all day long, and the king's daughter grew lonely being alone so long. As the night approached, she began to fear roving vagabonds, and worried whether the man would even return. He could have been involved in some kind of accident.

"Oh, dear, why didn't I pay attention to that emperor's handsome son?" she sighed. "Although, when I stop to think about it, my future husband is handsome too. . .if only he had some good clothes! But why didn't I accept the emperor's fine son? Although I do have to admit that my intended is better than that emperor's son. Oh, why did I refuse the rich emperor's son?"

Very late, the emperor's son returned. In a clay pot he brought some cabbage for his intended bride, and in a bag he had some bread and herrings. She ate them all, and was happy.

One day the emperor's son told his intended bride, "I have just finished making many clay pots. Tomorrow there will be a fair in the city and you will have to sell those clay pots there."

The emperor's son purchased many clay pots and also a tent. He set her up in the tent to sell the pottery. But secretly, he had hired 10 vagabonds and told them, "Run to the tent and smash all the seller's pottery!"

The men ran to the tent and smashed all of the king's daughter's pottery. The king's daughter ran, crying, to her future husband.

"Oh, my dear Sweetheart," cried the king's daughter. "Ten vagabonds ran into my tent and smashed all that expensive pottery!"

"That's what often happens to the poor. You just have to endure it."

"Aren't you angry with me, my Darling?" asked the king's daughter.

"No."

"How kind you are to me!" exclaimed the king's daughter.

They continued living in their hut, but one morning the bridegroom groaned and moaned, and said, "I am really quite sick this morning and will not be able to work today. I'm afraid we will now starve to death."

This frightened the king's daughter.

"Are you ill, my Dear? You stay here at home, and I will go to the emperor's castle to look for work and to bring you medicine, food, and drink."

The king's daughter left, but she had gone only a short distance from the hut when the emperor's son jumped up in very good health indeed, dressed, and ran quickly to the city before the king's daughter arrived.

The king's daughter reached the castle and began looking for work. The emperor's son, dressed in his royal clothes, was in the courtyard to greet her, and the king's daughter thought, "How good looking my sick sweetheart is! If he could only get clothes as fine as those the emperor's son is wearing, he would be just as handsome as the emperor's son. But it's useless to think of fine clothes now; if I can only make my bridegroom well!"

The king's daughter curtsied low and asked, "Could I get some kind of work here in the castle, for my bridegroom is ill and needs medicine and food."

"Do you care a lot for your bridegroom?" questioned the king's daughter's bridegroom.

"Of course I care for him. He has taken care of me for a long time with much love."

The emperor's son gave a short laugh, and asked, "But do you really know how to work? You look too delicate to do any kind of work. For instance, your hands are just as soft as those of my friend, an arrogant princess."

The king's daughter blushed a deep red and was afraid the emperor's son would begin to ask for her name and lineage.

But the emperor's son just said, "If you feel you

are able to work, you may serve as the castle's washerwoman."

The laundry work was hard and heavy for the king's daughter. Her delicate, white hands wore down so they bled. The hot water wrinkled them. But she worked hard, and when evening came and she was paid, she ran first to the pharmacy to buy medicine, then she went to a shop to buy food, and at last reached home, where the emperor's son, as a sick man, waited for her.

The bridegroom was ill for a long time, and the bride worked hard washing clothes in the castle.

The longer the bride took care of her bridegroom, the more beloved he became. But at last the king's daughter was worn out and ill from all her overwork. She said to her bridegroom, "I cannot stand much more. Let us die together."

The man answered, "No indeed. I don't care to die. You've got to struggle until I get well. But we still have some things we can try to do. Go to do the laundry one more time and steal the empress's silk blouse. Sell it, so we will get a lot of money. Then we can be ill together."

This suggestion frightened her, but in the end she agreed and said, "I will do anything that you ask me to do."

The king's daughter walked painfully to do the wash one more time and hid the empress's blouse in her bosom. But just at that moment, the emperor's son appeared and shouted, "What are you doing, Girl? Why, you are stealing my mother's clothes! I will see that you are fired from this job."

The king's daughter burst into tears. "Oh, how much evil I must have done in this world since I am now being punished so harshly. And it is true that I have done much wrong."

The emperor's son asked, "And what other wrongs have you done besides this one?"

"Oh, my good Sir, I can't even begin to tell you!"

"Just tell me," requested the emperor's son. "If you tell me, then I will forgive you this time, and you may keep your job."

"Oh, dear, it's so awful! I am the princess who had your horse tarred and shaved!"

"Is that so?" responded the emperor's son. "You do look quite a bit like her. And now I would like to show you . . . but I did promise to forgive you."

The king's daughter walked back to their hut, and the man asked, "Did you get the blouse?"

The king's daughter answered, "Let us die together. The emperor's son knows that I am the one who ridiculed him."

"No doubt you are feeling sorry that you have me instead of the emperor's son. Did you get the blouse?"

"I don't care for the emperor's son. I love you, not him. You have been so good to me. As for the blouse, I didn't get it."

The emperor's son now thought to himself, "Enough is enough."

Early the next morning the king's daughter went to the castle one more time to try to find work. The emperor's son met her at the castle gate, dressed in his handsome royal garments, and he said, "Do you know that today is my wedding day, and I need many workers to prepare for the wedding celebration. Since I have already once forgiven you, and since I don't really care very much for you, it is fitting that you go to help the kitchen maid this evening to prepare the wedding feast for my bride. Since you are poor, you will get the same wages as the other hired girls."

The king's daughter thanked him, but thought to herself, "Who would ever have thought that I would be hired kitchen help to the bride whose husband I ridiculed?"

When the wedding feast began, the king's daughter was busy in the kitchen serving as a helper to the kitchen maid. The emperor's son secretly sent someone to set fire to the potter's hut. Suddenly, someone ran into the kitchen yelling to the king's daughter, "Your hut is on fire, your hut is on fire!"

In her fright, the king's daughter dropped and broke a large plate of delicacies, and shouted, "Oh, how unlucky I am; my sick bridegroom is burning up!"

The king's daughter ran to the burning hut and would have rushed into the middle of the fire to rescue her bridegroom if the emperor's son had not held her back, saying, "It is I who is your bridegroom!"

"No, no you aren't! My bridegroom is a potter and he's burning up!" argued the king's daughter.

The king's daughter would not believe him until the emperor's son recounted all their experiences together. He told her how he had enticed her with the golden spinning wheel and the large doll to leave home, how they had struggled together. He told her all the things she had shared with the potter. After the emperor's son had explained all this, the king's daughter fell into his arms, and cried, "You will tease me no longer!"

"No, I won't," answered the emperor's son. "But now let us go to the castle, put on your wedding clothes, so we can celebrate our wedding."

So joy came at last to the king's daughter, even though she had prepared food for the bride— for her own wedding. The wedding was celebrated, and word was sent to her father.

The Little Sweetheart

Once upon a time a boy had a sweetheart. One day his little sweetheart said to him, "Build us a small cottage so we may live together there."

But the boy answered, "How can I build a cottage? Luck has not given me any money."

The girl said, "I will not remain your little sweetheart if you do not build us a cottage."

This made the boy very sad. That night as he slept, he heard a voice say in a dream, "Listen carefully, my Boy. Go into the wilderness until you reach a little hut. In that hut Luck is sleeping in a bed under a cover of green netting. Wake up Luck and ask him for money so that you can build a cottage and live there with your little sweetheart."

The next morning the boy went into the wilderness and walked until he reached a small hut. Luck was asleep in the hut under a cover of green netting. The boy tugged at Luck until he woke up and then asked him for money.

"Listen carefully," said Luck. "Keep on walking in the wilderness until you reach a deep pool. Copper, silver, and gold fish are swimming about in that deep pool. Fish for them, sell them, and then build a small cottage."

And so the boy kept on walking in the wilderness until he reached a deep pool. Huge jagged rocks formed the shores of the pool. The water was like the water in a deep well— it was as black as pitch. And yet, every now and then a fish as bright as a copper penny leaped above the surface of the water.

The boy sat down on a large rock and began to fish. His fishhook had barely dropped into the water when a small copper perch seized it. The boy pulled the perch in to the shore and rubbed it with his fingers to see whether the fish was a live perch or a valuable fish of copper.

It was a copper fish all right. Every fin and scale were made of pure copper. The boy was very happy and quickly hid the perch in his pocket and once more threw his fishing line into the water.

Just at that moment, a strange voice rose from the water, "Do you wish for more fish like that one?"

Badly shaken, the boy looked around, thinking someone had come to talk to him. When he saw no one, he gave a short laugh at his fear, and thought. "Why should I listen to such nonsense! Did I really hear something? And do I have to be satisfied with just one perch? I can't build much of a cottage with only one fish!"

"Of course I want more," he repeated silently over and over to himself. Finally he called out cheerfully, "Of course I want more!"

He caught many copper perch, but then he pulled in a silver carp.

Now the boy was overjoyed.

"Can this really be true?" he wondered. "Is this pool going to give up fish of silver? This is really something! I'm going to throw my hook into the water again."

He threw his hook into the water and again he caught a silver carp, shining like the blade of a knife. He was so excited that as he tossed his line into the water again, he kept jumping up and down for joy. The boy threw the copper perch on the rocks and filled his pockets with silver carp.

"Do you still want more of that kind?" boomed a dreadful voice from the water. Startled, the boy stood still.

"Whose voice can that possibly be?" the boy wondered. "Is it time to be really afraid?"

He would have been frightened, but suddenly he pulled a huge gold pike out of the water. The boy was speechless with joy. He scratched the pike; he bit its back to see if the fish was real gold. His teeth grated against the fish. It was gold, all right— pure, reddish-yellow gold.

Under the enchantment of everything that had happened, the boy grew pale and trembled. He now tossed all the silver carp aside and squeezed the gold pike between two large rocks, placed a third rock on top, and then seated himself on this rock.

"So you can't escape!" he reasoned. "I can get ten times more money for that one pike than from all the perch and carp put together!"

Just then a voice thundered so loudly from the water that the waves splashed high against the rockbound shore and small stones clattered down the steep, rocky sides.

"Do you want more of this kind of fish?"

The boy's heart throbbed with fear, just as if it had been struck with a hammer. The fishing pole fell from his hands. He intended to leave his fish and flee, but then the thought flashed through his mind, "I have a little sweetheart. If I don't take at least the copper fish with me, I cannot build our little cottage."

68

He decided to take only the copper fish with him, but then another thought flashed through is mind, "Why don't I take all the carp instead? With them, I can build a real house!"

He tossed the copper perch aside, planning to take the silver carp, when still another thought flashed through his mind, "While I'm at it, I might as well take that large, gold pike. With it I can even build a manor house!"

He now tossed aside the carp, intending to take the pike, but then yet another thought flashed through his mind, "As long as I'm going to build, why don't I build a palace of gold? I'm not afraid any more. I'll just throw my hook into the water once more."

He threw out his line. The sun was shining, the water was calm, and the wings of the dragonflies whirred and shone like brass.

The boy caught many, many gold fish. He threw all the copper and silver fish back into the pool and he soon sat on a large heap of golden pike.

Just then the strange voice pealed out like thunder so the water shot up into the air in a long column, pine trees on the rocky slopes crashed down, and the forest swayed before the boy's eyes.

The voice boomed out, "Do you wish for more of the same?"

At that moment the boy peered into the lake to see just what it was that boomed out like that. He peered down and saw a dreadful face on the surface of the water— its eyes were sunk deep into its skull, its beard was white, the head was bald, the teeth were broken.

"Phew! How ugly you are, Guardian of the Waters! I'm leaving now!" said the fisherman, and he filled his knapsack, his pockets, shirt, and hands with golden pike and ran homeward.

There he searched everywhere for his little sweetheart, but he did not find her anywhere.

He met a man on the road and the fisherman asked, "Where is my sweetheart?"

"Phew! How ugly you are!" shouted the man and he ran away.

"What, ugly am I?" the fisherman asked and, without getting an answer, left to search again for his sweetheart.

He came to the door of a small hut, knocked on the door, and asked, "Where is my little sweetheart?"

A voice from within answered, "I don't know your sweetheart, but I also had a sweetheart and fifty years ago he went into the wilderness to ask Luck for money."

"I was the one who went to ask Luck for money. I am your sweetheart. Please open the door, my little Sweetheart!"

"I will not open the door!" answered the voice from within. "For I already have another sweetheart!"

"Open the door!" cried the man. "My knapsack, my pockets, and the inside of my shirt are filled with large, golden pike. I will sell them and build us a palace of gold."

The door was opened but the one who opened it was not the fisherman's little sweetheart. She was an old woman. The door was opened, but then quickly shut again. The old woman called out,

"Phew! How ugly you are! I will not come to your golden palace!"

The fisherman called back, "Phew! How ugly you are! You are not my sweetheart. I don't want you in my palace!" And the man left to search again for his sweetheart.

He searched and searched for a whole week. At last he went back into the wilderness, walked until he reached a small hut. In the hut Luck lay in his bed under a cover of green netting. The fisherman woke Luck up and asked, "Where will I find my little sweetheart?"

Luck, in turn, asked him, "Did you fish in the deep pool and then build your little cottage?"

The fisherman replied, "I did fish there, but I did not build a little cottage. I plan to build a large palace."

Luck said, "I did not ask you to build a large palace! You will never find your sweetheart!"

With this, Luck yawned, turned over on his side, and fell asleep again under the cover of green netting.

The White Snake

A young farm hand inherited 30 pennies from his mother and he thought, "Now that I have received my inheritance, such as it is, I don't care to remain a farm hand any longer. I will, instead, go out into the world to seek my fortune."

And so he stepped out into the world.

As he walked along the road, he met a man who was carrying a cat in his arms.

The boy asked the man, "Where are you taking that cat?"

The man answered, "To the river. This cat is a thief and has done 10 pennies worth of damage, so he must be drowned."

The boy said, "Don't take him to the river! I will give you 15 pennies for him."

The boy then gave the man 15 pennies, and the man gave the cat to the boy.

The boy continued on his way along the road, the cat in his arms, until he met a man beating a dog. The dog was a stray. The boy ran at once to help the dog, and pulling the rawhide whip from the man's hand, he began beating the man, and said, "How does this feel? Why were you beating the dog?"

The man answered, "This dog is a thief, and since it has done 10 pennies worth of damage, it must be hanged. But since it doesn't come willingly to be hanged, it must be whipped."

The boy said at once, "Please do not hang this dog. I will give you 15 pennies for him."

The boy dropped 15 pennies into the man's hand, and the man gave him the dog.

The boy continued walking along the road, the cat in his arms, with the dog following behind.

All of a sudden, he heard a piteous cry. "Help me!"

The boy rushed toward the cry, and when he reached a huge, forked tree, he saw that a large, white snake had fallen between the two forks. The tree swayed in the breeze, tightly squeezing the snake. Unable to free itself, the snake called out with a heart-rending cry, "Help me!"

"I cannot bear to see any living thing suffer like this," said the boy to himself. He left the cat at the foot of the tree, climbed up and spread the two limbs of the tree apart and freed the snake.

The white snake said to the boy, "I would become your servant just as the cat and dog seem to be, but since there is a curse between man and snake, I cannot yet become your servant. But if you will follow me, you will be rewarded for your good deed."

So, with his cat and his dog, the boy followed the snake. The boy walked along the road and the snake glided in front of him.

They came to three forks in the road, and the snake blocked off two of the forks with its body so the boy could not enter either of them. But the snake permitted him to enter the third fork. Walking along the road, they finally reached an old castle that had been reduced to ruins during wartime. The roof was now covered with moss. The castle had a rusty entrance gate, and the snake slipped under the gate into the castle. Suddenly, the gate opened by itself, and the boy with his cat and his dog entered the castle.

Inside was a high, bright entrance hall, and the snake glided up some steps, and the boy followed. They reached a large door, the snake slipped under the door, and immediately the door opened by itself and the boy walked through. The boy kept following the snake until they reached a large room. All of a sudden, the snake disappeared, and the boy had no idea where it had gone. He looked all around the room. By now he was very tired since he had experienced much that day and had walked many miles. He would have liked to sit on a chair to rest, but there was not a single chair in that large room. Well, no sooner had he thought about a chair, than a door in the room opened by itself, and the boy saw a new, even larger room, with a golden, comfortable-looking chair. The boy entered the room, sat on the golden chair, and now thought, "If only I had something to eat."

The boy had just barely thought about food, when a door in the room opened and through the door slid a golden table, filled with the choicest of delicacies. The boy ate hungrily and also fed his cat and his dog. When they were all through, he thought, "I'm getting sleepy. If only I had some leaves and hay on which to lie down."

This thought had barely entered his mind, when a door in the room opened and through the door the boy could see an even larger room. He entered it and saw a beautiful, golden bed with a feather cover. He dropped into the bed and slept soundly for many hours.

When he awakened, a bright door opened in the wall and the boy saw a huge hall which shone like the sun and glittered with gold and silver. The hall was filled with huge snakes that were sliding along the walls, on the statues, along the roof beams. Their scales shone like the scales on the silvery bleak fish. At one end of the room the white snake was reclining on a beautiful rug. It was wearing a red cockscomb just like a rooster's, and it said to the boy, "Don't be afraid! Please come in. You saved my life. Now I wish to give you a reward."

So, with his cat and his dog, the boy entered the huge hall, and all the snakes bowed down to him. Hissing sounds filled the air.

The white, red-crested snake asked the boy, "What would you like as your reward? You may choose either me or a gold ring which will grant your every wish whenever you look through it and merely think of your wish."

As the snake was speaking, it developed arms and legs; its mouth became sweet and small; its eyes turned blue and bright; hair grew on its head. The snake had changed into such a beautiful young maiden that the boy could not take his eyes off her.

"I was bewitched into a snake, and only once a week do I become a human," the young girl said. "Which do you wish as your reward, me, or the gold ring?"

The boy, of course, desired the maiden, but he was frightened that only once a week would she be human. And he also wanted the gold ring.

Finally, he said, "What would I do with such a beautiful girl as you, for I do not even have enough money to take care of myself, my cat and my dog. I would like the gold ring."

The girl was somewhat disappointed, but she slipped the gold ring off her middle finger and gave it to the boy.

The boy with his cat and his dog now stepped happily down the castle stairs, and walked to the old iron entrance which opened before them. He reached the sun-drenched country road and walked along it with his cat and his dog. By noon he was tired and sat down on a small knoll beside the road. He took the ring off his finger, held it between his thumb and forefinger, peered through it at the sun, and thought about delicious foods.

"Let some food, some good-tasting food, appear here," he thought, and at once before him, as if they had dropped from a tree, were pasties with egg butter, porridge with syrup, and sweet milk in a wooden tankard. Now life was worth living! He ate and drank to his heart's content, while the cat and the dog watched hungrily.

"Of course there is food for you, too," the boy said and once again he peered through the ring, saying, "I wish for a pitcher full of thick cream and a large leg of lamb." Immediately, both of these appeared. The cat, with arched back, lapped up the cream, and the dog feasted on the large leg of lamb.

With his cat and his dog, the boy now walked to an inn to spend the night. Instead of ordering food from the inn, he now ate and drank his own favorite foods and shared them with his cat and his dog. Nor did he care to sleep in the best bed the inn provided; instead, he requested a gold bed with the help of his ring.

It so happened that through the window some thieves saw him enjoying his delicious foods, and they also noticed the bed of gold. When the boy had fallen asleep, they entered his room, intending to beat him to death. The boy was awakened by the noise, but still drugged with sleep, he couldn't, at first, understand what was happening. But then he remembered his ring, looked through it in the dark, and shouted, "Send seven men to help me!"

At once the room was flooded with light, and seven dark men appeared with flogging whips in their hands. They beat the robbers so hard that the robbers gladly released their hold on the boy.

The boy slept peacefully through the rest of the night, sleeping until late into the next day. He planned to continue walking onward when he suddenly thought to himself, "Why should I wear myself out with walking? We should have two silver-haired horses, a carriage made of gold, and a coachman dressed in a gold and silver striped uniform."

He raised the ring before his eyes, looked through

it, and immediately before him stood a shining carriage, horses, and a coachman who sat erect and handsome on the coach box.

With his pets, the boy climbed into the carriage, and the coachman asked, "Where does my master wish to go?"

To be honest, the boy really didn't know where they should go, but he replied, quitely rashly, "Why don't we drive to the emperor's palace?"

They drove so fast that the dust whirled up from the road. Before long the boy saw the gold towers of the castle, and in no time at all they were at the emperor's gate.

"I should really go to the emperor as a suitor and ask for his daughter as my bride," the boy thought.

Many a handsome prince had come to propose marriage to the emperor's daughter, but the emperor had considered none of them wealthy enough or worthy enough and had them thrown into a dungeon deep in the middle of the sea.

With his gold ring, the boy now disposed of his horses, his carriage, and the coachman and, dressed in his hired man's working clothes, he went to speak with the emperor and asked for his daughter's hand in marriage.

"Hohoo! How could I possibly give you my daughter when you are a mere beggar and of poor background?" said the emperor. "If only you had the same kind of castle and servants as I have."

"Wait until tomorrow morning," answered the boy, and he left the castle.

The castle faced a large sea, and the next morning when the emperor awakened and walked to his window, he saw, shining across the sea, an unbelievably huge castle made of gold, silver, and other precious metals. The emperor sailed to look more closely at the castle, and there, dressed in his poor man's garb, was the boy who had visited him the day before. Servants, dressed in uniforms trimmed with gold and silver, were serving that boy.

"Now will you give your daughter as my bride?" asked the boy.

"Ohoo!" exclaimed the emperor. "It is a miracle how you have produced this castle, but how can I possibly give my daughter to you? But, if in one night you can build a bridge of glass from one castle to the other so straight that it does not have even a one-inch bend in it, and also, if along both sides of the bridge you erect 12,000 statues, and on top of each statue you place a gold likeness of a human being, who speaks Russian, then I will give you my daughter."

"Wait until tomorrow morning," said the boy.

The emperor was awakened the next morning by the sound of many voices chattering, and when he walked to the window to look out, he saw a bridge of glass that stretched across the sea from his castle. The bridge was so straight that it didn't have even a hair's breadth of a bend in it. Also along both sides of the bridge stood 12,000 gold statues and at the top of each statue stood a brilliant likeness of a human and these were competing against each other in speaking Russian.

The emperor harnessed his horses in front of his carriage, with plans to drive across the bridge to look and to listen. But in taking their first steps, his horses slipped and stumbled on the glass bridge, and the emperor stepped out of his carriage and on his stomach began to crawl forward. But in his attempts to move ahead, his legs and hands took him backwards, and he did not even get on the bridge. The boy, driving horses, now came to meet him. His horses ran like the wind, for they had been shod with diamond horseshoes. The nails, made of diamonds, actually sliced off slivers of glass from the bridge; his horses whinnied; and the humans on the statues were still competing in speaking Russian. The boy lifted the emperor into his carriage and permitted him to drive to the golden castle.

"Now will you give your daughter to me as a bride?" asked the boy.

"Oh ho!" answered the emperor. "I will give her to you, but only if in one night you are able to erect two churches of glass at both ends of each side of the bridge. The bell towers must be of gold. All the bells must be ringing, a large crowd must fill the church, and the cantors should all be singing."

"Wait until tomorrow morning," said the boy.

When the emperor awakened the next morning, he heard the clamor and clang of many bells and when he stepped to the window, the gold-colored steeples of the churches shone like so many suns. Eight churches stood at the ends of the bridge, four of them near each shore. A red cloth had been spread along the road and on the bridge, and many beautiful ladies carrying parasols and gentlemen carrying canes walked along this red cloth—indeed, more ladies and gentlemen were walking there than the emperor had ever seen. From all the churches resounded the chanting of the cantors.

"The time has come for a decision," thought the emperor. "Must I now give my daughter to that hired man, who is of the lowest class?"

The emperor now put his daughter in a cell, behind eight locks and commanded his soldiers to seize the boy's churches, his bridge, his castle, and to imprison the boy.

But the boy looked through his gold ring and thought, "Let those 12,000 Russians jump down off their statues and toss the emperor's soldiers off the bridge and into the sea."

The boy now drove with his carriage along the glass bridge and he took his gold ring off his finger and thought, "Free the emperor's daughter from behind those eight locks to sit beside me in this carriage."

And the emperor's daughter did appear, just as if she had dropped out of the air.

There was nothing for the emperor to do now but to give his daughter to the boy as a bride.

The engagement party walked along the glass bridge from the boy's castle and 3,000 musicians played on golden flutes, and the guests walked into the churches made of glass, and the cantors sang.

The emperor disliked the boy intensely and yet he was jealous of him since the boy was of such poor birth, and yet he was so rich. The emperor could not understand how the boy could have accomplished all the miracles.

The emperor said to his daughter, "Ask your bridegroom how he managed to get the castle, the bridge, the churches, and you. Then come and tell me."

And so the emperor's daughter asked her bride-groom, "How did you manage to get the castle, the bridge, the churches, and me?"

The boy answered, "I have a special kind of ring. When I look through this ring and think about something I want, then I get it immediately!"

The emperor's daughter told her father, "He has a ring that he looks through and whatever he wishes comes true."

The emperor now wanted to steal this ring from the boy. One night, as the boy slept with the ring on his finger, the emperor sneaked in to steal it. But the boy woke up, looked through his ring, and cried out, "Ahaa! Let seven men come here to tie up this thief in a large sack and toss him into the sea!"

At once, seven dark men appeared; they stuffed the emperor into a flour sack, and started to toss him through the window into the sea. The emperor was frightened, begged for mercy, so the boy freed him from the sack.

The emperor now said to his daughter, "Try to get your bridegroom to give you the ring. He comes from such a low class that he isn't fit to be your husband."

So the bride begged for the ring, but the boy would not give it to her. But the boy had become suspicious, so when he went to bed, he took the ring off his finger, placed it in his mouth so it could not be stolen.

But that clever daughter of the emperor kissed the boy at night, and the ring slipped from the boy's mouth to her mouth.

She ran at once to her father and gave him the ring. The emperor lifted the ring close to his eyes, peered through it toward the moon, and said, "Send the boy into the tower deep in the sea, where the other suitors have been thrown. Tie him up in iron chains!"

The boy now sat as a prisoner in an iron dungeon in the middle of the sea. Sunlight never entered the dungeon through its one tiny window. In the base of the dungeon lay the bodies of the other suitors whom the emperor had considered too poor or of too low a class, and who had died here from starvation.

It looked as if the boy would also die from hunger in this deep dungeon. But after he had been lying down for one night and one day in the darkness without once getting out of his cell, he heard a cat mew and a dog bark near the only window.

The dog barked again and called down, "How are you getting along down there, dear Master? You are to be killed, but we will try to save you, for you saved our lives and have taken care of us. The cat jumped on my back at the shore and urged me to swim as fast as I could to try to help our master. So I entered the water and swam here with the cat on my back. What should we do now, dear Master?"

"I really don't know what you can do," answered their master. "But if you could get my gold ring from the emperor and his daughter, that would be of great help. Then I would not need to stay here among the dead for much longer."

The cat jumped on the dog's back again and the dog slipped into the water. The cat held on to the dog's neck with his claws, and the dog swam so quickly to the emperor's castle that the foam frothed below his chin. By night they had reached the castle, and when everyone in the emperor's castle had gone to bed, the cat slipped quietly into the emperor's bedroom through the crack below the door. He left the dog waiting outside the door. The cat searched the tables, dressers, and the tops of all the cupboards, but he could not find the ring. Around midnight the castle rats began to rustle around in the corners.

"Ahaa!" thought the cat as he began to stalk the rats. At last, he caught the largest rat in his claws and began to threaten him, "I'm going to kill you!"

The poor rat wailed and cried, "Please don't kill me!"

The cat replied, "Unless you go at once to find my master's gold ring, I will kill you and all the rats in the whole kingdom!"

"I will go to get the ring if you don't kill me," promised the rat.

The cat released the rat.

The rat slipped under the bridge and whistled all his brothers and sisters together. They all entered the emperor's bedroom and began to gnaw at the dressers and cupboards but nowhere could they find the ring. They also called all the mice in the castle together and forced them to hunt for the ring. But they could not find the ring anywhere.

The rats and the mice were frightened when they saw the cat's eyes gleaming in the corner. But suddenly, a white ant, which had been rustling and chewing along a crack in the wall, remarked, "The ring is not in the chests or the cupboards. It is in the mouth of the emperor's daughter!"

In the emperor's room, the smallest mouse ran to the window sill, which held a large box of snuff. This little mouse took a pinch of snuff into its fingers and ran to the daughter's room. It ran up to the bed and stuffed a little snuff into one nostril of the emperor's daughter.

"Atshish!" The emperor's daughter sneezed so hard that her mouth opened wide, but the ring was not in her mouth.

"Then it is in the emperor's mouth!" cried the white ant.

The largest rat hurried to the emperor's bedroom, filled both hands with snuff, ran to the emperor's bed and stuffed snuff up both of the emperor's nostrils.

"Hutshish!" The emperor sneezed so hard that his mouth opened wide and the gold ring tumbled onto the bedspread.

The rats and mice were overjoyed to see the ring. The biggest rat handed the ring to the cat, and the cat patted the rat's forehead with his paw, saying, "Now you are king of all the rats!" And ever since, a cat does not care to eat a rat, even though he kills it.

When the people in the castle began stirring the next morning, the cat did not dare to mew to be let outside, for he feared the ring would drop from his mouth. So the cat patiently waited beside the door until someone would go out, and he could slip outside.

"What a remarkable cat! It's so well trained that it doesn't even mew in the house," said the emperor as he opened the door for the cat. The dog was waiting outside. The cat signaled with his paw that they must leave at once to swim to their master. The cat jumped on the dog's back, the dog plunged into the water, and they began their trip toward the island with its prisoner.

The dog swam so fast that the foam frothed below his jaw. Only after they had reached the high seas did the dog dare to ask the cat, "Did you get the ring?"

"I did!" mewed the cat, but then the ring dropped from the cat's mouth into the sea.

"Oh, you gap-toothed cat! You can swim on your own now!" And the angry dog pushed the cat off his back into the water.

"Why didn't you ask me while we were on shore?" responded the cat.

The ring was now lost somewhere in the deep water, and the starving boy was waiting for them in the dungeon. But how could they find the ring in the water?

Angry at each other, the cat and the dog climbed up on an isolated islet in the middle of the sea. As they walked along the islet looking for food, the cat saw a huge pike on the shore. He clutched the pike's neck in his claws, and said, "I'm going to kill you!"

"Don't kill me!" begged the pike. "What do you want for not killing me!?"

Now the dog began to bite at the pike.

"What do you want from me? What can I do, so you won't kill me?" the startled pike asked.

The dog replied, "A gold ring has just fallen into the sea. Would you go and look for it?"

The pike promised to look for the ring and with a splash he slipped into the water. He swam after sunfish, perch, and roughy, and asked each of them, "Have you seen a gold ring?"

"We haven't seen anything like that," answered the sunfish, the perch, and the roughy.

But one little roughy said nothing. It seemed a little sly and began to swim away. But the pike had noticed him and said, "Ahaa, you little Rascal! I see you bristling your spines. Have you seen the gold ring?"

The pike grabbed the young roughy by the neck and shook him so violently that the roughy cried out, "Yes, Yes! I have seen a ring like that. It was like a small band."

"Ahaa!" shouted the pike. "Is that right? You have swallowed that ring! Cough it up!"

There was nothing for the roughy to do but to give up the ring.

The pike swam up out of the water and gave the ring to the cat and the dog. Both of them were over-joyed. But all at once the cat and the dog began to quarrel. Who was going to carry the ring?

The dog said, "Let me carry it, for your teeth are so far apart that you will drop the ring into the water again."

And so they fought. The dog bit the cat. The cat, regardless of how he spat and clawed, finally proved weaker than the dog. So the dog got to carry the ring.

Once again, they began the trip to the dungeon. They moved right along, with the dog feeling very satisfied, but with the cat feeling sulky as he sat on the dog's back. They swam for a long time; the sun was shining, and the water reflected the sunshine. All of a sudden, many small fish glimmered brightly near the surface of the water. The dog saw them and thought the ring had dropped from his mouth and was now shining in the water. He snapped his jaws to get the ring back in his mouth, but the ring, which really was in his mouth, fell into the sea. The cat hissed to the dog, "Didn't I tell you, you with your drooping jaw!"

What should they do? There was nothing for them to do but to go back to their rocky islet. In the meantime, their starving master kept waiting for them.

Once again the dog and the cat got hold of a pike. They sent him off to find the ring, and again the pike retrieved the ring from the bottom of the sea.

Once again the cat and the dog swam toward their master. The cat sat near the dog's neck, and the dog swam so fast that the foam frothed below his jaw.

"Swim faster, you Lazy One. Our master is in need, in need!" repeated the cat.

The dog was tempted to answer in anger, but he dared not, for the precious ring was in his mouth.

At last the cat and the dog reached the dungeon in the middle of the sea, where the boy was a prisoner. The cat took the ring from the dog, and with the ring in his mouth, climbed to the very top of the tower, and from the one window the cat called down to the boy, "I will drop the ring; be sure to catch it!"

The boy grabbed the ring as it fell through the air, hurriedly peered through it, and yelled, "Away with my chains! Let us have dancing and music!"

The walls of the dungeon crumbled down, the boy's chains fell apart, and a large group of violin players and whistlers sat among the ruins playing and whistling.

Peering through his ring, the boy shouted, "Let all those who have died rise up again!"

At once, all the suitors who had died of starvation awakened from the ruins, all of them healthy and full of life.

A merry dance began now that the boy had been rescued from the dungeon and death. They all danced, the boy, the revived suitors, the cat, and the dog. When the boy had had his fill of dancing, he sat down on a large rock to rest and to eat. He now took the ring off his finger, gazed through it, and made a wish, "Will the white snake please come here?"

In a moment, the white, red-crested snake stood before him.

"What do you wish?" asked the snake.

"I wish you would take back this ring," answered the boy. "I prefer to choose you, even if you remain a snake for seven days out of every week. This ring can bring much bad luck as well as good luck."

As soon as the boy finished speaking, the white snake changed into a beautiful young girl. She was so beautiful that the boy almost fainted.

The young girl said, "The spell has been broken. I was bewitched to live as a snake until a man would come who would select me rather than the gold ring. Never again will I turn into a snake. Take me now."

"I will, I will take you!" answered the boy.

Just then a large ship with sails of gold and silver stripes sailed to the rocky island and the maiden, the boy, with his dog and his cat, embarked on the ship and sailed away to the snake's magnificent castle.

The Crown of
Diamonds

Of four brothers, three were hardworking and diligent, but the fourth was so lazy that he was called lazy Aatukka.

When the four brothers went into the forest to slash and burn trees to clear land for farming, three of the brothers worked hard all day long so that perspiration dripped off their shoulders, but the lazy brother just sat on a rock near the land being cleared and wiggled his bare toes in the warm ashes.

The older brothers scolded him for not helping, but Aatukka simply remarked, "I would be industrious if I could only find my kind of work."

In the evening when they started for home, the three brothers began to walk, but Aatukka was so lazy that he didn't feel like walking. No, Sir! From the burnt clearing he took a partially burned, many-forked stump, and straddling it as if he were riding a goat, he pushed himself along with two sticks, just as if he were skiing— simply because, you see, he didn't want to walk.

The next day the brothers returned to continue their slashing and burning. Dripping with perspiration, the three worked hard among the stumps, but the youngest brother just sat on a rock and wiggled his toes in the ashes.

It so happened that a devil's* son was sitting in a large birch tree in the middle of the land being cleared. As the flames shot upward, the birch leaves turned yellow, and began to burn. The slant-eyed devil's son began to choke from all the smoke and was about to burn. He peered down from the tree, and begged, "Boys, please put out some of your fires so I can get down!"

"We don't have the time!" shouted the three brothers, and they continued even more energetically to pry up the stumps.

"Let me come down, please let me come down, so I can run off into the forest! I will pay you well!" cried the devil's son, but the busy brothers didn't pay any attention to him.

So now the devil's son called down to the lazy brother, "I'm beginning to burn up! Listen, Aatukka, free me from this burning perch, and I will pay you well!"

Lazy Aatukka jumped up and said, "This may just be my kind of work!"

Aatukka tore many branches off a spruce tree, dipped them into the water of a nearby ditch, and

*devil, in Finnish, *hiisi*, in the pre-Christian era could mean a "guardian of the forest."

92

beat the stumps burning below the birch. He snuffed out the flames and the devil's son clambered down the trunk of the birch and laughed merrily, for now he was freed. He took a small whistle from behind his ear, and said, "Here is your reward, Aatukka. You will need it!"

The devil's son then disappeared into the forest, and Aatukka was left standing below the birch tree, the whistle in his hand. Later, he often blew on it for his own amusement.

It so happened that in the kingdom the daughter of the diamond-crowned king was being wooed by many suitors. Her father, the king, had recently died. Aatukka's three older brothers decided to go woo the king's daughter.

"Well, here again is my kind of work!" decided lazy Aatukka, and he also went to woo the king's daughter.

The diamond-crowned king's daughter lived in a castle on a high mountain. But not once had she yet showed herself to her many suitors. She demanded heroic deeds from them, and those who could not perform these difficult deeds had their heads chopped off, which were then placed on the pickets of a fence surrounding the castle. This picket fence seemed almost to reach the clouds. Only four pickets on the fence remained without heads.

And so the brothers arrived to woo the king's daughter. They were warmly welcomed at the castle and were served pasties, a tasty porridge, and were given mead to drink. But the lovely daughter of the diamond-crowned king did not appear.

The time arrived for the performance of the deeds, and the king's daughter sent word to the brothers through her maid, "I will not appear until the victor comes. However, I believe that he will never come. Whoever cannot perform the heroic deeds will have his head chopped off, and it will be placed on a picket in the fence."

The brothers all asked, "What, then, are these deeds we must accomplish?"

The maid answered, "The king's daughter has a huge, gold-horned ox in the stable. When the ox is released to go into the forest, the suitor must follow him, and when he returns in the evening, the suitor must bring with him some grass from the exact place where the ox has eaten and water from the spring from which the ox has drunk. Each suitor must go alone with the ox into the forest, and on the day assigned to him."

The ox was released from the stable, the oldest brother was handed a bottle, and he followed the ox into the forest. The ox was huge, his coat dark red, and his horns as thick as a man's arm. For a long time the ox bellowed and stamped about on the meadow, butted his head against the trunks of pine trees, and kicked dirt, which landed on his back. All of a sudden, he stopped all this romping, raised his head, opened his jaws, and gave a great bellow. Quickly, he ran into the thick forest, with the brother following behind. The ox ran over hills and into valleys, he waded through swamps and creeks, but not once did he stop to eat or drink. Finally, he reached an enormous rapids, where the water shot up high into the sky. For a while the ox walked calmly back and forth on the shore, as if looking for a place to cross. Suddenly he plunged into the turbulent water at the crest of the rapids.

"Now that crazy ox will kill himself, and I certainly don't dare to follow him!" the oldest brother said to himself.

The top of the rapids shone in the sun, and the ox was tossed about like a dry log. He swam toward the falls, where he gave a hoarse bellow, and fell headlong down into the rushing rapids and disappeared from sight. Not even his horns were visible in the foaming water.

"Now he has drowned!" thought the oldest brother.

But wait a moment. After a while, at the foot of the rapids, the head of the ox appeared, then his back, and finally, the ox itself climbed to the other shore. He shook the water off his body, glanced behind him, gave a shrill bellow, and ran into the forest.

"He didn't drown!" moaned the brother. "And now he has escaped from me! Where can I find the grass from which he will eat and the water from which he will drink? I will try to outwit the royal household. I will lie in wait near the castle, and when the ox returns home, I will gather some ordinary grass and take ordinary water, walk behind the ox to the castle, and offer both the grass and the water to the royal household."

And so the oldest brother walked to the meadow near the castle and waited. In the evening when the ox walked out of the forest, the brother filled the bottle with water from a spring below the meadow. He then grabbed some grass beside the spring and walked to the castle with the ox.

The royal household asked, "Did you bring grass from the spot where the ox had eaten and water from the spring where he had drunk?"

"Yes, I did!" assured the oldest brother.

"Well, we will soon see if you're telling the truth," he was told. "Bring the grass and the water here. If the ox eats and drinks of them, then they are the right ones."

The grass was offered to the ox, but he just sniffed at it and did not eat any. The water was also offered, but he did not care for that either.

"You dared to lie to us!" he was told, and so the hired men took hold of the oldest brother, led him to a pine chopping block, cut off his head, and placed it on one of the pickets in the fence.

The other two brothers wept over this, but lazy Aatukka just reflected, "There's nothing we can do about it now."

The following day, the next to the oldest brother followed the ox. When they reached the shore of the rapids, he clung to the ox's tail and plunged into the rapids with the ox. But the ox thrashed about so much in the rapids that he completely wore out the brother. When they both rose out of the rapids to the other shore, the man was so exhausted that he didn't have the strength to run after the ox as he ran into the forest. The man fell sound asleep on the shore. When the ox returned to the rapids in the evening, the brother pulled some grass from the shore and stuffed it into his pocket. He also filled the bottle with water from the rapids. The ox swam across the rapids, with the man hanging again to his tail. They reached the castle, where the grass and the water were offered to the ox. The ox ate a few blades of grass and sucked up only a little of the water.

Now came the pronouncement from the household, "Oh, you poor Man! You didn't have the strength to stay with the ox. Your head should really be chopped off, but we will, instead, show you mercy. You are to sit in a dungeon for half of your life."

And so this brother was locked into the dungeon. The next to the youngest brother cried bitterly, but lazy Aatukka just thought, "There's nothing we can do about it!"

The following day, the next to the youngest brother followed the ox into the forest. Hanging on to the ox's tail, he flew across the rapids and ran after the ox through a large forest. A lovely sunny meadow filled with white and yellow daisies suddenly opened before them. Small knolls, on which gold grass was growing, rose up among the daisies, and water as bright as the sky circled the bottoms of the knolls. The ox took a bite here and there of the gold grass growing on the knolls, and whenever he had taken a bite, the ox drank a little of the water at the base of the knoll from which he had eaten the grass.

"I'll be sure to win the girl with the diamond crown!" rejoiced the next to youngest brother as he pulled some gold grass off a small knoll and stuffed it into his pocket. At the base of another knoll, he filled his bottle with water.

That evening he walked home with the ox. When the ox was offered the gold grass, he ate half of it, but left the other half. He was offered water; here again the ox drank half the bottle, but left the rest.

97

It was now pronounced to the next to the youngest brother,"My poor Man, you were close, but not close enough. You should be killed, but we will show you mercy and offer you another chance in a new test."

Now the youngest brother, lazy Aatukka, left the next morning with the ox. Everything went well and they reached the meadow in the forest where the gold grass grew and the bright water shimmered in the sun. Whenever the ox bit off grass from a knoll, Aatukka took some grass from that knoll. He did the same with the water, taking some water from every pool from which the ox drank.

Aatukka reached home with the ox. When the grass from Aatukka's pocket was offered to the ox, he ate the grass eagerly, his tail wagging. When the ox was offered the water, he drank the water so fast that the ox snorted through his nostrils.

So lazy Aatukka was now told, "You have done very well. But a new test will now begin for you, one that is not easy."

"What kind of test is it?" asked Aatukka.

"This is the test: The king's daughter has 300 rabbits in a large sheepcote. You and your brother, each one working alone, will have to herd the rabbits in the forest for one day and bring them home at night. However, if even one rabbit is missing, your head will find a place on the fence picket."

"Well, I guess we'll just have to try the test," said Aatukka.

The next morning the door to the rabbit pen was opened, and the next to youngest brother was the first to serve as the shepherd. Three hundred rabbits hopped out of the pen. They ran wildly about the grounds, and when the castle gate was opened, the rabbits rushed into the forest and spread out in all directions like ashes in the wind.

During the whole day, the next to the youngest brother ran here and there, panting and puffing, but he was not able to catch a single rabbit. In the evening, he arrived at the royal household alone, and sad.

"Did you bring the rabbits?" he was asked.

"They're all still in the forest," he answered.

"You poor Man!" he was told. "Your head should be chopped off and placed on a fence picket. Instead, you are to spend half of your life in our dungeon."

"Well, there's nothing to be done about that," thought Aatukka.

When the sheepcote was opened the next morning, all of the rabbits were there. They were released, and Aatukka became the shepherd. The rabbits once again disappeared, like ashes in the wind. Aatukka searched everywhere— among the rocks, within the clumps of willows, around the haystacks, but he did not see a rabbit anywhere. He was downhearted. He ran here and there, and shouted at the rabbits, he shrieked at them, and he even called gently to them, but not a single long-eared rabbit came to him. All day long he searched, and by evening, without the rabbits, he walked toward the castle, thinking, "Now I will be beheaded, or sent into the dungeon for half of my life. And nothing can be done about it now!"

Aatukka repeated to himself, "There's nothing to be done." And he put his hands into his pants pockets, walked along, whistling and carefree, when his hand happened to touch the whistle the devil's son had given him. For his own amusement, Aatukka began to blow on the whistle.

He had blown the whistle just once, when suddenly the forest came alive— it began to move; it jumped, it rustled, it whirled. From the forest 300 rabbits rushed toward Aatukka with such force that he almost fell to the ground.

Blowing merrily on his whistle, Aatukka led all the rabbits home. Great joy filled the castle; the people shouted and cheered.

"A man has come here who has a magic touch. Now we shall have a wedding!"

The people celebrated the wedding for three weeks, but the king's daughter had not yet showed herself to her bridegroom.

But, finally, at the end of the last day of the celebration, the king's daughter appeared before Aatukka. She was not at all pretty, and she was quite small. There was little beauty in her and her skin was gray. Furthermore, she was not wearing a crown of diamonds but wore only a copper crown.

Aatukka said, "You have deceived me! But there's nothing that can be done about that now."

The king's daughter answered, "I have not deceived you, but I carry a great sorrow. Three years ago, my dear sister, my oldest sister, disappeared. If you can bring her back here, I will be extremely happy and will turn beautiful once more."

For some time, Aatukka thought about how he could bring the oldest sister back home. After thinking for a long time, he finally blew on his whistle. The sound was loud and shrill. Pushing their way into the room through the doorway, the wise ones of the forest entered; they were red-haired, red-tailed foxes.

"What do you want?" asked these wise, grinning foxes.

"What I want to know," answered Aatukka, "is where my late father-in-law's daughter disappeared to three years ago. I must bring her back here. What must I do?"

"What you must do now," said the foxes, "is to follow us to a faraway wilderness. A desolate mountain rises in that wilderness and a giant named Jymy lives within that mountain. Often, when we have chased partridges, we have come to the top of Jymy's mountain, and we know that your late father-in-law's daughter is inside the mountain."

Following the foxes, Aatukka ran toward the wilderness. The foxes ran fast, their red tails streaming behind them. At last they reached the mountain. It was dark, but one light flickered in an opening in the mountain. Aatukka crawled through the opening into the mountain, and there in a cavern, the giant Jymy sat cross-legged beside an enormous fire, roasting a whole elk. The giant's eyes glared with cruelty, his beard bristled like the needles of a pine tree, and his lips looked like hams smoked to a dark brown.

"Who are you?" the giant asked Aatukka.

"I am Aatukka and I am looking for the late king's oldest daughter. Can it be that she is here?" asked Aatukka.

"Yes, she's here," answered the giant. "She is in one of the back rooms. But you cannot have her until you play blindman's buff with me. I will be the blind man first and will give you a bell to hold in your hand so I can hear where you are. When I catch you, I will eat you, but if I do not catch you, you may take the king's daughter."

Jymy, the giant, tied a band made of elk leather over his eyes and gave Aatukka a bell. They began to play blindman's buff. Aatukka blew on his whistle and out of a crack in the wall, a rat jumped into Aatukka's hand.

The rat whispered to Aatukka, "Give me the bell and you slip into that large hole in the wall!"

So Aatukka slipped into the large hole in the wall while the rat began to ring the bell and to jump about the room. Jymy heard the ringing of the bell, and thinking that Aatukka was ringing it, he stretched out his huge hands toward the sound, but he could not even touch the rat, for it always escaped into its crack in the wall. Finally, Jymy was worn out and said, "Let's rest awhile and then play again."

Aatukka jumped out of his hiding place, took the bell from the rat, and the rat slipped into his own hole. Jymy pulled off his elkskin blindfold, and rested.

When he had rested, Jymy again put on his elkskin blindfold; the rat jumped into Aatukka's hand, took the bell into his paws, while Aatukka slipped into his hole in the wall. Jymy lunged at the rat but could not catch him. Again Jymy grew tired. Aatukka came out of his hiding place, took the bell from the rat while Jymy removed the blind-fold from his eyes, and rested. They played blindman's buff three times, but Jymy could never catch Aatukka.

"Well, you may as well take that king's daughter!" said Jymy, and he opened the door to the inner room where the king's daughter was sitting. She was overjoyed when she saw another human being.

Aatukka took his bride's oldest sister home, where his bride met them on the portico. She was now more beautiful than she had been before. She was smiling and wearing a crown of silver.

"You still are not wearing the crown of diamonds," said Aatukka.

His bride replied, "I will wear the crown of diamonds when you bring my second oldest sister back here. She disappeared two years ago."

"Where is your second oldest sister?"

"Nobody knows!"

Aatukka blew on his whistle and in no time at all, the forest's wolves gathered about him.

"What do you want, King Aatukka?" they asked.

"I want to bring back my father-in-law's second oldest daughter, but I don't know where she is."

"Jump on my back," said one of the wolves.

Aatukka sat on the back of the strongest wolf, a yearling. He hung on to the wolf's neck hair and they moved so fast through the forest that the wind whistled in their ears and sparks flew from the wolf's claws, sparks brighter than the eyes of the wolf.

At last, they saw flames blazing like the northern lights near the top of a mountain. As they drew near, they could see on the mountain a church made of clear glass, with many lights burning inside.

"We have reached the devils' special place, the forest's remarkable church," said the wolves. "The

103

late king's second oldest daughter is sitting under the altar, guarded by devils. Slide off my back, my King, and take the woman from under the altar, while we wait outside."

Aatukka climbed up a golden ladder into the church where the devils, dressed in gaudy clothes, were walking back and forth, chanting while the late king's second oldest daughter sat under the altar and wept.

The biggest devil approached Aatukka, bowed low, and asked,"What is it you want, Stranger?"

"This stranger wishes you to give him what is sitting under the altar weeping," answered Aatukka.

"Is that so? You can, of course, have her, but what can you give as ransom?"

"I don't have much to offer," said Aatukka. "But I do have a whistle with which you can call together all the four-legged animals within the forest."

"If you give us that whistle, you may take the king's daughter right away," replied the devils.

Just as Aatukka started to hand over his whistle, a devil's little son jumped out of a pew and shouted to the most handsome of the devils, "Do not, dear Father, take that whistle from this boy! He once saved me from the middle of a blazing clearing. Dear Father, give him the girl for nothing!"

All those in the church were filled with joy when they heard that Aatukka had once rescued a devil's son from the middle of a burning clearing. A banquet was held in Aatukka's honor, and afterwards, 300 wolves were harnessed to a golden carriage. Aatukka and the rescued girl sat in the carriage. In no time at all, they arrived at the castle.

Aatukka's bride was overjoyed when he arrived

with her sister, but she was not yet wearing the crown of diamonds. She wore only a crown of gold, and her arms were covered with gold beginning at her elbows and her legs from the knees down were also covered with gold.

"Aren't you ever going to get the crown of diamonds?" asked Aatukka.

"Don't be angry!" answered his bride. "I will certainly get the crown of diamonds when all my sorrows have disappeared. A year ago my youngest sister was bathing at the seashore when an ogress rose out of the sea and pulled her down into the water. If you bring her back, I will place the crown of diamonds on my head."

"I must try to rescue her," said lazy Aatukka.

Aatukka walked to the shore of the blue sea, where the sun was shining and the sea murmured as if it were filled with pieces of gold. Aatukka blew on his whistle and with much splattering and splashing, all the seals in the sea rushed from the water. Soon the shore was filled with long lines of wise, bewhiskered seals, all merrily flapping their flippers.

"What do you want, old Aatukka?" the seals asked.

"What I want is my father-in-law's youngest daughter, who was kidnapped by an ogress. How can I rescue her?"

"Sit on our backs!" answered the seals.

Aatukka sat on the back of the heaviest seal, which had red fins, like those of a perch. All the seals plunged into the water, and Aatukka dived right along with them under the surface of the water.

Aatukka could not hold his breath for very long under water, but the seals kept diving ever deeper, and it grew ever darker the deeper they all swam in this realm of the water god. At last green mountains appeared, and it was easier to breathe. They entered the dwelling of the ogress, where they found the youngest sister of the king's daughter, looking very melancholy, lying down in a large room. She was guarded by a thousand codfish.

The ogress leaped up from her bench, stared viciously at Aatukka, and hissed, "What do you want?"

Aatukka answered, "I want that girl prisoner lying on that bench covered with perch bones."

"You cannot have her!" shouted the ogress. "Attack him, my Codfish!"

The codfish were just about to bite Aatukka with their spiny jaws, when Aatukka said to the ogress, "Won't you give me the girl if I give you a whistle with which you can call together all fish, and everything that swims?"

This offer pleased the ogress very much and she said, "If you give me that whistle, you may have the girl. I will even take you and the girl home."

Aatukka gave his whistle to the ogress and she hitched a thousand codfish to a gold, canopied carriage. She slipped gold bits into the mouths of the codfish. She herself sat up on the coach box and began to drive. Aatukka and the girl sat in the carriage under the gold canopy, which, like a moon, gave off light inside the carriage. In such style did Aatukka ride home.

But just as they entered the royal grounds, Aatukka saw a horseman mounted on a black horse galloping away with such speed that the ground trembled. The horseman was holding Aatukka's bride, who was moaning and weeping. But on her head she was wearing the crown of diamonds, which sparkled like the stars in the sky.

"I am doomed, for I gave away my whistle!" Aatukka moaned as he left the rescued maiden on the portico of the castle, and began to run after the thief. He ran through swamps and fields, up hills and through forests, until he finally reached the brink of a rushing rapids. The horseman had also reached the rapids and was busy watering his black horse. The woman was waiting on the grass nearby. When the thief saw Aatukka coming, he looked at him with eyes full of hatred; then he laughed at Aatukka, took his gun off his shoulder, and struck Aatukka many times with it, and said, "You have conquered others, but you will not conquer me!"

He lifted the woman on the horse, and they fled across the surging rapids.

Lying prostrate on the grass with serious injuries, Aatukka lay close to death, but then he began to implore the Supreme God of the Ancient Finns, "Please send your golden birds, send your sweet honey bees before daylight, under the moon, send ointments in a gold cup to revive a dying man."

And the Supreme God of the Ancient Finns did send his golden birds, his gold cups before daylight, under the moon. The cups were filled with honey with which the wounded hero rubbed his injuries. Suddenly healed, Aatukka rose up from the ground and continued his quest for the thief. But no boat was on the shore of the rapids.

Aatukka leaped into the water and swam across the raging rapids to the other shore. Lo and behold, just as he stepped onto the other shore, a golden archway appeared; within it were statues made of precious stones. Monkeys ran up and down the statues. As they climbed up, they sang melodic songs, and as they ran down, they told amazing stories. Through the archway, Aatukka saw a garden where golden apples were shining.

The hero walked through the archway into the garden, where golden cuckoos were singing on the golden apples. As he walked into the middle of the garden, Aatukka reached a beautiful castle, a kind of castle he had not seen even in his dreams. The porticos were made of gold, all the eaves were of precious stones, and golden swallows were singing below the eaves.

As Aatukka stepped up on the portico, the king's daughter came out of the castle, more beautiful than he had ever dreamed she would be. Her skin was white and smooth. Her arms were covered with gold and her legs, from the knees down, were also covered with gold. On her head the crown of diamonds twinkled like the stars in the sky.

She was his bride, the king's daughter. They now began their life together and joy filled the golden castle.

The Merchant's Son

Once upon a time a merchant's son went into the forest to hunt. He hunted all day, but did not get to shoot his gun even once. By evening his dogs had vanished into the dusk. The merchant's son sat on a rock in a meadow to rest and to eat some berries. All at once from the edge of the meadow he heard the sharp barking of dogs. He began to walk toward the barking, thinking, "What are the dogs barking about? If I could only manage to shoot something!" He reached the edge of the meadow but did not see the dogs anywhere even though the barking was close at hand. He looked to the right and there, on the top of a tree stump, he saw two pairs of dogs' jaws, just white bones on the stump, barking so the whole meadow resounded. At first the merchant's son was filled with fear, but then he gathered up his courage and slipped the dogs' jaws into his pocket. The barking ceased immediately.

"It's getting dark," he thought. "I must go home before the forest becomes more haunted. My dogs can come home later."

The merchant's son gazed at the stars to discover the direction he should take to find his way home. Then he began walking quickly toward home. Suddenly from the forest came the sound of the most beautiful music, violin music.

"Now what is happening?" he wondered as he was drawn toward the lovely sound. As he approached the music, he saw a violin on top of a stump, playing all by itself.

"I'm not afraid of this, either!" he thought, and put the violin inside his shirt.

Once again he started his walk homeward. It was now pitch dark. Suddenly he noticed a bright light twinkling far in the forest.

"What cottage can that be?" he wondered. "It is now too late to continue homeward. If that light is coming from a cottage, then I will spend the night there."

He walked toward the light, which grew larger and brighter. Finally, he stood before a huge house where the weather vane, the well sweep, and even the swinging buckets of the well were made of gold. Bright lights were shining from the windows. The boy saw no one in the yard. He stepped up to the veranda. No one came to greet him, so he opened the door. He saw a woman placing meat in the oven to roast.

"You poor Soul!" she said. "You have strayed into a wicked place. This is the House of Giants and when the giants get home they will kill you."

"Where are the giants now?" asked the boy.

"The men are in the forest hunting game and the women are out dancing, but when they get home they will kill you."

"So they'll kill me, but who are you?" the boy asked.

The woman replied, "I am a human being and will do you no harm. I was kidnapped to become a slave here."

As the woman was speaking, the boy pulled the two dogs' jaws out of his pocket and took the violin from inside his shirt, and asked the woman if she knew what they were.

"Why, those are our men's hunting dogs and the

violin belongs to our women. Since they will be searching for them until early morning, you may stay here for the night."

The woman then brought good food and drink to the table, and fed the boy well.

After the boy had eaten they went to look over the house, and the woman led him from room to room. They opened the bronze door at the back of the house and entered a room in which bronze treasures dazzled their eyes. From there they opened a silver door and silver lamps blazed upon silver chests. Then they opened a golden door and gold in large heaps glowed like the red-hot irons in a smithy. At the very end, they reached a door which shone as brightly as the sun. But the woman did not open that door.

"Why won't you open this door?" asked the boy.

"I have been firmly warned not to open it, and I will be banished from this house if they see that I have opened it. My life here at the House of Giants is a good life. I will not open the door."

But the boy insisted. "Open it anyhow," he said. "As long as we don't go inside they will not know that we have peeked in through the door."

"They will be sure to know. But since you are such a handsome boy and you ask me so nicely, I will open it if you give me those dogs' jaws which you found in the forest."

"Here they are," said the merchant's son as he gave the barking jaws to the woman.

When the woman turned the key in the lock, the door flew open. The merchant's son was blinded at first. He almost fell over backwards in his shock over the amazing sight that met his eyes. A mirror hung on the back wall of the room and on the mirror was a portrait of a beautiful girl. She was so beautiful that drops of blood flowed from the boy's lips as he thought about kissing such a girl.

All night long the boy sat cross-legged on the floor of the room, gazing at the picture. No matter how she tried, the slave woman could not get the boy to leave the room.

In the morning the giant family came home from the forest. There were men as tall as pine trees and others as short as dwarfs. There were ugly women and beautiful women, all dancing gracefully. But they were all in an ugly mood.

"What is wrong with my masters?" the slave woman asked.

"All day long we hunted for game and did not find any, and finally even our dogs vanished into the forest. We hunted for them all night, but did not find them."

"And what is wrong with my mistresses?" asked the slave woman.

"Our music disappeared into the forest in the middle of the dance. We hunted all night but did not find it. And now here at home we can smell a Christian!"

Then the men approached the slave woman. "It smells of a Christian here," one of them said. "You have hidden an outsider here."

The women began to search. They searched and searched but did not find the merchant's son. Then the men began to search. They searched and searched and found the merchant's son in the farthest room, sitting before the girl's picture. They accused the slave woman, "You have unlocked the forbidden door! Now you will have to leave this house!"

But the slave woman said, "If you don't drive me away I will find your dogs for you."

This pleased the giants very much, and she was told, "If you find our dogs we will not drive you away."

The slave woman gave the dogs' jaws to the giants, and they told her she would be permitted to stay.

Meanwhile, the women had gone to the boy. "Why did you come here?" one of them said. "We'll kill you!"

The merchant's son answered, "If you don't kill me and also give me that picture, I will give you back your violin."

This pleased the women, and he was told, "Give us our violin right away and we will not kill you. And we will also give you the picture."

So the boy gave them the violin and he left the house in peace, taking the picture with him.

The merchant's son returned home, kept the picture on the wall during the daytime, and at night he kept it beside him as he slept. During the day he gazed constantly at the picture, and at night he dreamed about it. One night during his dream, the picture came alive and said, "If you wish to see me as I really am, journey at once into your neighboring kingdom."

The next morning the boy asked his father for six beautiful ships filled with costly treasures to sell. His father gave him the ships and the son set sail across the blue sea to the neighboring kingdom to sell his treasures in a foreign land. The wind carried his ships to the other side of the sea— to a shore of sea shells, to a shore of pearls, to a golden shore, where a huge palace glittered in the sun.

Beyond the palace lay a foreign city, a city teeming with people of many kinds. The merchant's son moored his ships at the emperor's wharves, and under a red fabric tent on the deck of one of his ships he began to sell his treasures. There were tankards of gold, silver bowls, earrings, silver shoes. There were swords made of gold and hats of gold. There were sparkling liquors in shining bottles.

The boy was kept busy selling. Large crowds visited the ship; the people were handsome; they bought many of his treasures. Whenever he sold something, the merchant's son offered the buyer a drink, often giving it as a gift.

One day a sea captain came to buy a blue jacket, a seaman's jacket. The boy gave him the blue jacket, did not ask him to pay for it, and as a final gesture, treated the captain to a drink. As the sea captain mellowed, he became talkative and the boy led him down to his cabin, where the picture of the beautiful girl beamed from the wall, and he asked, "Captain, do you know whether there is a girl like this anywhere in this kingdom?"

"Alas, my poor young Merchant, what are you thinking of? Yes, there is a girl like that who lives close by, but whoever utters her name will have his head chopped off!"

Now the boy began to draw out the sea captain. "Please tell me about her. I will not let anyone know what you say! I will give you much gold!"

And so the sea captain began, "Since you are such a handsome lad and gave me a jacket, drinks, and everything, and will also give me gold, and since you have promised not to tell anyone what I tell you, then I whisper to you: She is the daughter of our emperor!"

114

"How can I get to see her?"

"Oh, ho, you poor Merchant! It is not easy to see her. The emperor keeps her inside the palace, closely guarded. But once a month she is allowed to go for a sail on the sea."

"Couldn't I see her then?"

"Well, perhaps you could, but that would be dangerous. I am the captain of the ship on which the emperor's daughter sails. I have a thousand able seamen guarding her. But I can remove one of them and let you take his place. If you give me much gold, you will be able to look at the emperor's daughter."

The young merchant gladly gave the sea captain much gold, and the captain made him an able seaman on the emperor's ship. After a month had passed, the emperor's daughter went on a pleasure trip on the sea, and the merchant's son was on her ship. While land was still in sight, the emperor's daughter did not come up from her cabin, but as soon as the land had disappeared from sight, she came up on the deck. The eyes of all the seamen had been covered with handkerchiefs. The merchant's son's eyes were also covered, but the captain had covered his eyes with such a thinly woven handkerchief that the boy could see right through it. The boy looked at the emperor's daughter and almost swooned. She was so beautiful that drops of blood broke from his lips; oh, she was beautiful! When he felt the blood begin to trickle from his lips, the boy wiped them with the kerchief. The emperor's daughter looked at the boy as he wiped his lips and at once fell deeply in love with him. She invited the boy down into her cabin and withdrew the handkerchief so she could see his eyes. And when she had seen them, she begged, "My dear Seaman, please give me the handkerchief as a memento, for I am becoming very fond of you."

The merchant's son gave her his handkerchief and she, in turn, gave him her own handkerchief bearing the emperor's crest and her initials. And then they also exchanged rings.

By this time the sea captain had concluded that nothing good could come of this— that the emperor's daughter had even invited the merchant's son into her cabin!

"When the emperor hears of this, he will have my head chopped off!"

So he went to speak to his seamen, "If any one of you even mentions that one of our seamen went into the emperor's daughter's cabin, he will be put inside a nail-studded barrel and tossed into the sea. Isn't that the right punishment, Boys?"

"Yes, Yes!" shouted the seamen. "For even a sailor should be permitted to go into the emperor's daughter's cabin!"

Nevertheless, the sea captain told the merchant's son, "I have now fulfilled my promise; you have seen the emperor's daughter. I can no longer permit you to remain on board this ship— not at any price."

Sadly, the merchant's son left the ship.

The next time the emperor's daughter went on a pleasure sail, she came up on the deck just as soon as the ship had left the shore. She looked around for the sailor with whom she had exchanged rings on the last trip. She looked and looked, tried to smile, grew frightened. The sailor was not on the ship. Disappointed, she became ill and returned at once to her cabin. She gazed at the sailor's ring and

116

at his handkerchief, on which the drops of blood shone like pearls. She cried bitterly, this daughter of the emperor. Finally she called the captain to her cabin and said, "I am not feeling well. Let us turn homeward; the sea is rolling so much today."

The ship was turned homeward and they sailed back to the shore of pearls, the shore of sea shells, the golden shore, and the emperor's daughter was taken to the palace.

The emperor's daughter now lay ill in her bed, languishing, pining away from loneliness. Her suffering was so great, it was hard to understand. The emperor was overcome with sadness now that his daughter was ill. He summoned all the doctors to the palace, but not one of them could make her well. She became seriously ill. The emperor sent a thousand messengers to announce to the whole kingdom that magicians, sorcerers, knights, even beggars, were invited to come to cure his daughter. And whoever made his daughter well would win her and half the kingdom.

This was exactly what the merchant's son had been waiting for, as in his sorrow he sailed over the seas, gazing at the emperor's daughter's ring, her handkerchief, and her picture.

He dressed in beggar-magician clothes and re-turned to that shore of gold, that shore of pearls, that shore of sea shells. He went to the palace and told the emperor that he could make his daughter well.

The emperor, who could not understand his daughter's illness, was filled with great joy and gave the merchant's son gifts of all kinds and built a golden sauna, in which the "magician" was to treat his daughter. In the sauna, this charlatan

117

cooked in a golden pot, cooked in it over the heated stones. He announced that he was concocting medicine, although what he actually was making was just sugar water. He boiled it for a long time and then called the emperor's daughter into the sauna.

She did not recognize the merchant's son in his beggar's clothing and said, "Your medicines are all in vain. They will not make me well. Nothing will make me well!"

"At least try this medicine!" requested the "magician", and the girl drank it. The sugar water was so hot that beads of perspiration broke out on her forehead. The "magician" pulled the emperor's daughter's handkerchief out of his pocket and began to wipe the moisture off her brow. His patient noticed at once that it was her own handkerchief!

"Where did you get that?" she quickly asked.

"My master gave it to me today," answered the merchant's son.

Eagerly she asked, "Where is your master now? Is he still alive? Is he well?"

The boy answered, "He is well. Indeed, he is very well!"

Then the girl said, "I am beginning to feel better already. Your medicine has really helped."

She now went to her father. "I am feeling much better now," she said. "That man had me drink such wonderful medicine."

The emperor was greatly pleased and awarded the merchant's son a splendid stallion.

The next day as the "magician" was again treating the emperor's daughter, he showed her the royal ring and said, "My master gave this to me today."

The girl begged, "My dear Magician, isn't there some way in which you could arrange a meeting between your master and me?"

The "magician" answered, "If you promise to be well by tomorrow, then my master will be here in my place tomorrow morning."

The girl was delighted and said, "I promise to be completely well when I come to see him tomorrow."

Very early the next morning the emperor's daughter came to the sauna and as she stepped through the door, there stood her seaman, resplendent in handsome merchant's ermine and wearing long chains of gold. She was so captivated by his appearance that she rushed to embrace him and cried out, "Oh, Dearest, here you are at last. I was so afraid that you were lost to me forever!"

"Now will you marry me?" asked the young man.

The emperor's daughter burst into tears. "I have been promised to the magician who made me well, even though it was not his medicine that cured me. I became well immediately upon hearing that I would see you once again."

Then the young merchant confessed, "I was the 'magician'!"

And when he opened his magnificent ermine coat, he revealed his beggar-magician's dress.

The girl said, "Everything is going to turn out all right now. Take off that handsome coat, wear only your magician's garb, and let us go to my father."

The young merchant left his handsome clothes in the sauna, and as a "magician" he went with the emperor's daughter to the palace.

She told her father, "I am completely well now.

This very wise man cured me and I wish to marry him."

At first the emperor was unhappy at the thought of giving his daughter to a poor magician. But then he observed, "I made a promise. The magician may marry you, and you may marry the magician, but I will turn the magician into a general!"

And in grand style the "magician" was made into a general in a sparkling church of glass, where hundreds of candles glowed and many torches gave off a sweet fragrance. After the "magician" had been created a general, he rose off his knees and said to the emperor, "I am not a poor magician. I am the son of a wealthy merchant from the neighboring kingdom across the blue sea."

And when they stepped out of the church, lo and behold: twelve gilded ships were just sailing toward the shore, the wind blowing against their purple sails. The ships glided to a stop at the shore, and the merchant's son guided the emperor toward the largest ship and said, "From the other side of the blue sea, my father sends these twelve sailing ships to the emperor who gave his daughter to a beggar and magician."

And great was the joy on that shore of pearls, that shore of sea shells, that golden shore!

A Difficult Situation

Once upon a time a man had to take a wolf, a goat, and a basket of cabbages across the river. But his boat was so small that only one of these three could be carried over at a time. This made for a difficult situation indeed.

If, for example, he took the wolf first, then the goat, left alone with the cabbages, would gobble them up. He could, of course, take the goat over first, for a wolf does not eat cabbages. But who would he take next? The wolf? Oh, no! For as soon as he left to get the cabbages, the wolf would immediately attack the goat. If he took the cabbages next, then the goat would gobble up the cabbages while he went to get the wolf. It was, in truth, a most difficult situation!

Scratching his head, he pondered over his problem. All of a sudden, the solution came to him. First, he rowed over with the goat. This left the wolf with the cabbages, which he did not touch. On the second trip, he took over the cabbages, but then he took the goat with him on the return trip. On the third trip, he took over the wolf, who did not care for cabbage. And for the last trip, he went back for the goat.

This is the way he solved his difficult problem.

Source: *Kuva-Aapinen (The Picture ABC)*, Finnish Lutheran Book Concern, Hancock, Michigan, 1912, page 23.

The Story of Folklore

The prose folklore of Finland includes tales, legends, myths, anecdotes, riddles, and proverbs. Folk tales were first told out loud, most often by country people.

As the tales were passed on from one generation to the next, the story tellers might change something, add something, or take something out, to fit their style of telling, their time and place, or their audience.

Most folk tales, regardless of country, follow a pattern: something is missing or needed; the quest, or seeking for whatever is missing, begins; magic often enters to help; some tests or trials must be passed; the reward is won; and the tale ends on a happy note. In folk tales, very often people who live in poverty rise to great heights; a poor peasant boy wins the king's daughter, half the kingdom, and half the kingdom's treasure.

Most of the stories in this book follow the traditional folk-tale idea, but some depart from pattern, ending in disappointment.

A distinguishing feature of many folk tales is that the characters do not have specific, given names; they remain the king's daughter, the king's son, the merchant's son, the youngest daughter, the oldest daughter, and so on.

All the tales in this book, except *A Difficult Situation,* are from the collections in the Folklore Archive of the Finnish Literature Society in Helsinki,

Finland. This archive is one of the largest of its type in the world, with almost 3 million manuscripts, 8,000 hours of recorded material, and 35,000 photographs—a rich source indeed for anyone interested in Finnish folklore.

Finland was a province of Sweden from about 1155 to 1809. Although most of the people spoke only Finnish, Swedish was the official language of Finland. In 1809, as a result of a war between Sweden and Russia, Finland gained a number of autonomous powers, and became a Grand Duchy of Russia. Use of the Finnish language inspired vigorous intellectual activity.

In 1831, the Finnish Literature Society was established. This Society helped to finance the collecting trips of Elias Lönnrot, a physician who made many journeys into Finland, Karelia, and Estonia to create a written record of Finnish folk poetry. Lönnrot developed it all into the epic *Kalevala*, which was published by the Society. A number of books have resulted from the collections of the Society. These include *Legends and Tales of the Finnish People* (*Suomen kansan satuja ja tarinoita*), by Eero Salmelainen.

One of the tales in this book, *The Namesake Trees, or the Mouse Bride,* was taken directly from the Salmelainen collection by Aune Krohn, whose collection was published in 1909 by the Finnish Literature Society, (*Suomalainen kirjallisuuden seura*).

Ten stories in this book are from *Tarulinna* (*The Castle of Tales*), taken originally from sources in the Finnish Folklore Archives by Joel Lehtonen (1881-1934) and published in 1906 by Werner

Söderström Oy., Porvoo, Finland. The artist who illustrated the book is Venny Soldan-Brofeldt, the wife of Juhani Aho (1861-1921), a well-known Finnish newspaperman and writer.

Source materials for this chapter included *Kai Laitinen, Literature of Finland, An Outline,* Otava Publishing Company, Limited, Helsinki, Finland, 1985, and A Finnish Literature Society Brochure, Helsinki, Finland, no date given.

I wish to thank Dr. Rudolf Jensen, Associate Professor, Grand View College, Des Moines, Iowa, for his general support which resulted in this book, for reviewing all the translations of the tales, and for sharing his knowledge about the world of folk tales.

— *Inkeri Väänänen-Jensen*

About the Translator

Inkeri Väänänen-Jensen (also known as Ingrid Jensen), is the daughter of Finnish immigrants who settled in northeastern Minnesota in the early 1900s. She began in 1973, at the age of 58, the serious study of Finnish language, literature, and history. She has degrees in English and Finnish from the University of Minnesota.

After six years of intensive work, she published *Finnish Short Stories*, translations of 32 stories by 19 of Finland's short story writers.

One chapter of her life story, *Inkeri's Journey*, still in manuscript form, was published in the book, *Sampo: The Magic Mill*, New Rivers Press, 1989. Three of her translations are also in *Sampo*.

Penfield Press published Inkeri's translations, *Finnish Proverbs*, in 1990.

She has collaborated with several other people on a book about Helmi Mattson (1890-1974), a Finnish immigrant editor, novelist, poet, essayist, and short story writer. This book is sponsored by the Immigration History Research Center, University of Minnesota.

Her latest work is this volume, *The Fish of Gold and Other Finnish Folk Tales*, for Penfield Press.

Inkeri is writing poems about her experiences as a child of Finnish immigrants, *Poems from Inkeri's Journey*. She has read from her writings at programs in Minnesota, Iowa, and Wisconsin.

Books By Mail

Prices are postpaid. 1990 prices subject to change.

The Fish of Gold and Other Finnish Folk Tales (this book), $9.95.

Finnish Proverbs, translated by Inkeri Väänänen-Jensen, $8.95.

Fantastically Finnish: Recipes and Traditions, 6x9 inches, 88 pages, $7.95, 2 for $15, 3 for $18.

Fine Finnish Foods, 3 1/2 x 5 1/2 inches, 160 pages. $5.95.

Please write for a complete price list.

Penfield Press
215 Brown Street
Iowa City, Iowa 52245